Engaging Children's Minds

Engaging Children's Minds

The Project Approach

Third Edition

Lilian G. Katz, Sylvia C. Chard, and Yvonne Kogan

 PRAEGER

AN IMPRINT OF ABC-CLIO, LLC
Santa Barbara, California • Denver, Colorado • Oxford, England

Library of Congress Cataloging-in-Publication Data

Katz, Lilian G. (Lilian Gonshaw), 1932-
  Engaging children's minds : the project approach / Lilian G. Katz, Sylvia C. Chard, and Yvonne Kogan.—Third edition.
    pages cm
  ISBN 978-1-4408-2843-0 (hardcover)—ISBN 978-1-4408-2872-0 (paperback)—
  ISBN 978-1-4408-2844-7 (ebook) 1. Project method in teaching. 2. Early childhood education. I. Chard, Sylvia C. II. Kogan, Yvonne. III. Title.
  LB1027.43.K38 2014
  . 371.3'6—dc23   2014017350

ISBN: 978-1-4408-2843-0 (cloth)
      978-1-4408-2872-0 (paper)
EISBN: 978-1-4408-2844-7

18 17 16 15 14   1 2 3 4 5

This book is also available on the World Wide Web as an eBook.
Visit www.abc-clio.com for details.

Praeger
An Imprint of ABC-CLIO, LLC

ABC-CLIO, LLC
130 Cremona Drive, P.O. Box 1911
Santa Barbara, California 93116-1911

This book is printed on acid-free paper ∞

Manufactured in the United States of America

Contents

Preface

Twenty-five years have passed since the publication of the first edition of *Engaging Children's Minds*. The second edition was published in 2000. For this third edition, we are joined by a third co-author, Yvonne Kogan, from Mexico City. We have been working with Kogan for 16 years now, writing, presenting workshops, and speaking at conferences together. We have learned much with her and from her through the project work she has supported in her school over the past 16 years.

Since those two earlier editions of this book, we have also had extensive worldwide experience of working with teachers who have been implementing the project approach, mainly with preschool and kindergarten children. During that time, it has become clear that teachers of both younger and older children are implementing the project approach effectively with many benefits to the children.

In this third edition, we have included a variety of examples of project work undertaken by children within the whole age range from toddlers to the upper elementary school levels. We have also discussed the important influence of the increasingly widely recognized practices in the preschools of the city of Reggio Emilia in Italy. Putting our experience and theirs together strengthens our commitment to supporting all children's capacities for query, observation, and representation of their thoughts and ideas in ways their teachers can support them.

Thus, for the third time, we are emphasizing that children should have a wide variety of activities that engage their minds fully and that support their natural quests for understanding their experiences and for acquiring knowledge, and that offer meaningful opportunities to apply the wide range of academic skills that must be learned, especially in the elementary school years, as well as when they are being introduced to children during the preschool years.

We look forward to opportunities to meet with you and hear from you and learn from you about your experiences of implementing the project approach with the whole age range of children we have suggested in this edition.

Acknowledgments

In this third edition, we acknowledge also the teachers and administrators of two schools in particular: Eton School, Mexico City, and Duke School, Durham, North Carolina. Yvonne Kogan, principal and co-owner, has been our contact with Eton School, where the teachers have been most willing to provide us with accounts of their experiences and photographs of children and their work. Kathy Bartelmay, the curriculum director at Duke School, has also been working with us for many years, and teachers there have been most generous in sharing their project work experiences with us for reference in this edition.

ONE

Introduction to the Project Approach

In this opening chapter, we outline the aims and benefits of including project work in the curriculum during the toddler and preschool through the elementary school years. Some of the major aspects of the project approach are highlighted as we begin with a brief look at project work in progress in an early childhood classroom:

Several kindergarten children are collaborating on a painting depicting what they have learned about various parts of their school bus. Their teacher is helping them label the steering wheel, horn, gearshift, the dashboard, ignition, accelerator, hand brake, brake pedal, turn indicators, windshield wipers, and the inside and outside rearview mirrors.

Another small group in the class is working on felt-tip pen drawings of parts of the motor, indicating where they believe the oil and water are put into it. The children make a diagram representing their understanding of how fuel flows from the gas tank to the motor and how the exhaust makes its way through the tailpipe. As they work, they correct each other and make suggestions about what goes where and what details to include.

A third small group is working with their teacher to prepare a documentation of their investigation of the bus. Their documentation will include drawings and paintings with labels and descriptions that will enable others to grasp their findings. The displays in the documentation will show the different kinds of lights inside and outside of the bus and which lights are for signals and warnings and which are used to light the way ahead as well as the inside of the bus. Some lights are red, some amber, and some white; some flash on and off and some are just reflectors.

Throughout the investigation, their work is accompanied by lively exchanges of information, questions, and opinions about what they have seen and how things work. They also discuss how to include all of their observations and findings in the documentation so that their classmates who worked on other aspects of their bus can fully grasp their message.

A fourth group of children has prepared a chart of the gauges and dials on the dashboard of the bus, providing a basic idea of the information each gives to the driver. As they work, they refer to the observational drawings they made of the dashboard while inspecting their school bus.

Two of the children in the class used a rope to establish the width and length of the bus. They have displayed their rope on a counter in front of a sign the teacher helped them to write:

Our bus is 2 ropes wide and 6 ropes long.
It has 8 wheels and 42 seats.

The children also take a moment to explain to an inquisitive schoolmate how they measured the bus. Earlier that day, they had described the data-gathering processes to the principal of their school when she visited their classroom.

Two children are completing a large illustration of the safety features on the bus. These include a fire extinguisher, emergency doors and windows, an emergency exit sign, and a first-aid kit.

Six other children are playing in and around a large model of the school bus constructed in the classroom. The heavy cardboard container painted in traditional school bus colors by the children includes the name of the school district, license plates, and other words copied down from the real bus during their field studies. A few rows of seats made of large blocks and small chairs, a steering wheel, and a rearview mirror stimulate the spontaneous, animated role-playing that includes a bus driver, traffic officers, and lively and noisy passengers.

Although this project involved the children in a detailed study of their school bus over a period of several weeks, the knowledge and skills gained and used are unlikely to be assessed on traditional standardized achievement tests. However, numerous state performance standards or benchmarks are addressed by most of the children in very meaningful ways in the course of their project work. Furthermore, the example illustrates the main thesis of this book: namely, that the inclusion of project work in the curriculum promotes *children's intellectual development by engaging their minds in observation, raising questions and predicting the answers, and conducting investigations and many other intellectual processes as they study selected aspects of their own environments and experiences in depth.* Ideally, they investigate those aspects of their environments worthy of their attention, understanding, and energy.

The special knowledge gained by the children about the nature of their school bus was not the only benefit of the project. The project also provided occasions for making careful observations, taking measurements, resolving disagreements, and developing explanations. It also provided real contexts for writing and other literacy strategies and many other important kinds of worthwhile learning that are discussed further in the following chapters.

WHAT IS A PROJECT?

We use the term "project" to refer to an extended in-depth investigation or study of a particular topic—uncovering as well as covering the subject of the study. Project investigations are usually undertaken by a whole class, with small groups within it working on particular subtopics. But the key feature of a project is that it is an investigation of a topic of interest and potential value to the learners. The investigation includes a wide variety of research processes and procedures that involve children in seeking answers to questions they have formulated individually as well as together and in cooperation with their teacher. Projects also usually include seeking answers to the many new questions that arise as the investigation proceeds.

Projects consist of exploring and investigating a topic, such as "building a house," "going to the hospital," or, as in the example above, an in-depth study of the bus that brings them to school. The topics of projects can vary widely, depending on the ages of the children and the environment in which they live. Implementing the project approach includes the same basic processes as classical science: a question emerges from discussion, for example, Where does our water come from?[1] The investigators share their hunches and guesses and predictions about what the answers to their questions might be. The investigators then come to agreement concerning what they want to find out and generate a list of questions about the topic. They then discuss what kinds of data they would need to obtain in order to be able to answer their questions and to check their predictions, as well as where and how they could obtain the needed data. They also share ideas about to whom to pose their questions, which experts to invite and to interview, and finally conclude the project by preparing detailed documentation that serves as a report of their findings.

We suggest that it works best when a project is conducted in three phases. The first phase consists of deciding on the topic to be investigated and the development of a list of beginning questions to find the answers to. It also includes the children's predictions of what the answers might be. In addition, suggestions are developed about possible sites to visit and experts to consult and objects to collect.

During the second phase of a project, the children follow up their research questions by conducting various kinds of field work and inviting experts on various aspects of the topic to their classroom to answer their questions. They also consult a variety of secondary sources of information on their topic, such as books, videos, local museums, Internet sites, etc. During this second phase, they also make a variety of representations of their new understandings of the topic and refine and elaborate the data collected as they make new discoveries.

The final phase or conclusion of the project usually includes inviting parents and others to see the completed documentation of their work. In this way, a class can share the story of their project and communicate with others what they have found out and learned. As already suggested, it is a good idea to keep in mind that rarely is project work the "whole curriculum." Rather, depending on the children's ages and school and district requirements, the total amount of time allocated to project work can vary, depending on the phase of the project and other requirements the school may have to meet at various times in the school calendar.

A project involving an in-depth study of the neighborhood, of some specific aspect or institution within it, or of the seasonal changes in local weather and its effects on neighborhood trees, etc., might be extended over many weeks or a few months. However, with the young children, a project might occasionally be completed within a week or two. Unlike spontaneous play, projects usually involve children in advanced planning and in various activities that require several days or weeks of sustained effort. However, brief, impromptu mini-projects might be stimulated by an unexpected event, a visitor, or an unanticipated event during a well-planned project. Impromptu, brief projects are most likely to work well with toddlers and other groups that include mainly the younger children in the program (See Kogan & Pin, 2009).

Work on a project usually extends over a period of days or weeks, depending on the children's ages as well as the nature of the topic under investigation. Preschoolers might spend two or three weeks on a hospital project; older children, on the other hand, might spend twice or three times as long on the same topic. Some of the projects undertaken by preprimary children in the Reggio Emilia municipal pre-primary schools in Italy extend over several months (See Gandini, Etheredge, & Hill, 2008; New, 2005)

At any age, children with a wide range of special needs can be encouraged to participate in a project. The teacher usually has a role in helping the others to think about good ways to involve those children with special challenges, abilities, and disabilities, and to help them with the work they are willing to try and able to undertake. In this way, the teacher helps all children to have meaningful and satisfying participation in the projects. Also, all the children can learn that the inclusion of peers with special needs is expected, that there are ways to facilitate their participation, and that it is also right.

THE PROJECT APPROACH IN HISTORICAL AND INTERNATIONAL PERSPECTIVE

The practices included under the term "project approach" are not new to early childhood or to education in general (Van Ausdal, 1988; Prawat, 1995). Stewart (1986) asserts that the idea of learning through projects originally gained popularity in the United States, where it was advocated by both Dewey (1904) and Kilpatrick (1918) and was generally included when using the term "progressive" education. It can also be seen in Susan Isaac's (1966) descriptions of children's work in England in the 1920s. The project approach also closely resembles the Bank Street curriculum model developed over many years at the Bank Street College of Education in New York City (Zimilies, 1997).

Project work was a central feature of the practices identified, described, and advocated in Great Britain in the document that came to be known as the "Plowden Report" (Plowden Committee Report, 1967; Department of Education and Science, 1978). British educators labeled them variously as the "integrated day," "integrated curriculum," and "informal education." During those years, hundreds of North American educators visited what used to be referred to as "infant schools" all over Britain to observe high quality project work. During the late 1960s and early 1970s, many Americans incorporated these methods under the title "open education" (See Gardner & Cass, 1965).

The complex reasons for the decline of progressive education at the end of the 1930s and of the open education movement in the United States in the middle 1970s and the "integrated day" in Britain in the 1980s cannot be taken up in any detail here. However, it is often noted that educational philosophies and ideologies, at least in the Western world, swing back and forth in pendulum fashion (e.g., Kliebard, 1985; Alexander, Murphy, & Woods, 1996).

From time to time, a particular approach to early childhood education is enthusiastically embraced and implemented. Within a few years, a counter-movement emerges, resulting in over-corrections in the opposite direction, only to be followed some years later by over corrections in reverse. It seems to be in the nature of education in general, and in the fields of early childhood and elementary education particularly, that opinions and ideologies concerning appropriate curricula and methods are argued with great heat and conviction by each generation of parents, educators, and politicians (Dearden, 1984; Katz, 1995).

Several factors may account for current re-introduction of and increasing interest in the project approach. First, an accumulating body of research on children's development and learning supports the proposition that good project work is an appropriate way to stimulate, strengthen, and enhance children's intellectual and social development, as well as strengthen their competence in basic skills (Blair 2010; Dresden & Lee, 2007).

Second, no evidence suggests that the project approach puts children's intellectual or academic development at risk. However, like any other innovation, curriculum, or teaching method, the effectiveness of the project approach depends on many qualitative factors, such as the selection of topics for projects as discussed and described in later chapters, and the skillfulness with which teachers guide and support the children's project work.

Third, we advocate the approach as *part of* a balanced curriculum throughout the preschool, primary school, and elementary years. During the preschool period, a large part—but not all—of the curriculum is allocated to spontaneous play. As children get older, increasing proportions of the curriculum are given to systematic instruction. We suggest that formal instruction and spontaneous play are not the only two alternatives for any age group. It is our view that in addition to these two kinds of activities, project work is an appropriate and substantial part of the curriculum throughout the preschool and elementary school years.

Finally, like many other educators of young children, we continue to be inspired, informed, and instructed by the variety of projects conducted by young children in the Reggio Emilia pre-primary schools. In particular, their detailed documentation of the children's experiences and ideas has provoked many educators to turn to projects as a significant part of the curriculum throughout the early and elementary school years.

At all age levels, project work provides contexts for careful observation, in-depth investigation, exchange of ideas, mutual support, cooperation, collaboration, resolving conflicts, seeking further information on the related topics, and other important experiences while in the process of learning about significant aspects in the world of people, objects, and events around them.

What Is the Project Approach to Teaching and Learning?

We use the term "project *approach*" for several reasons. First, it reflects our view that projects can be incorporated into the curriculum for all ages of learners in a variety of ways, depending upon the preferences, commitments, and constraints affecting teachers and schools. In some cases, project work takes up a large proportion of the curriculum, although not necessarily for the whole school year. In other cases, project work is offered just two afternoons a week. For others, especially at the preschool level, teachers devote most of the curriculum to it. In other words, there is no single way to incorporate project work into a curriculum or teaching style. The significant feature is that some time is allocated to experiences in which children make careful observations and inquiries into worthwhile events and topics over sustained periods of time.

Second, project work as an *approach* to early childhood and elementary education refers broadly to a way of teaching and learning, rather than to a set of specific teaching techniques, activities, or procedures. This approach emphasizes the teacher's responsiveness to the individual children as well as to all of the children in the class. On the basis of his or her special knowledge of the children, the teacher can encourage them to interact with people, objects, and aspects of their environment in ways that have personal meaning for each of them. As a way of learning, the project approach emphasizes children's active participation in the planning, development, and assessment of their own work; children are encouraged to take initiative and responsibility for the work undertaken, and it increases as children get older.

The topic of a project for young children is usually drawn from the world that is familiar to them and is frequently based on their expressed interests and curiosities. Thus, one might expect projects in a rural school to focus on the animals raised and the crops cultivated on the nearby land (Wilson, 1971). Children in a fishing village might be engaged in projects about boats, fishing, and fisheries. In an urban area, children can undertake projects about types of buildings, construction sites, factories, traffic patterns, vehicles, the shops on the nearby main street, and the variety of workers involved. Some projects can be developed when children collect data at home and bring their drawings and related objects into their classroom to share with others and prepare an overview of their findings. As children grow older, it will be highly appropriate for them to study other people, objects, and environments that are not within their own first-hand experiences but that are more distant in both time and space.

In principle, the younger the children, the more important it is that the topics they investigate have *horizontal* rather than *vertical* relevance. "Vertical relevance" refers to instruction and learning that is intended to prepare children for the next class or the next school; the former, "horizontal relevance," refers to learning content and activities that are meaningful at the time they are experienced. In other words, as children increase in age and the experience and competencies that accrue with age, it is the responsibility of schools to help them understand and know about phenomena distant from their own first-hand experiences. However, the major aims of education in the early years are (a) to strengthen children's confidence in their understanding of their own environment and experiences and (b) to support and strengthen what should become lifelong dispositions to seek understanding and knowledge of significant events and phenomena both near and far.

What Are the Aims of the Project Approach?

The overall aim of the project approach is to support and strengthen children's lively and growing minds. In its fullest sense, we use the term "mind" to include not just knowledge, understanding, skills, curiosity, and the dispositions to go on learning, but also social, emotional, moral, aesthetic, and spiritual sensibilities and understandings.

An appropriate education throughout the early years should address the full scope of children's growing minds as they strive to make better and fuller and deeper sense of their experiences. As they get older, project work can also support their efforts to make better and fuller sense of other peoples' experiences—people further away in time (history) and in place (geography). It encourages them to pose questions, pursue puzzles, and increase their awareness of significant phenomena around them. From four to about eight years of age, most children still respond eagerly to adults' suggestions, contribute readily to group efforts, and try out new skills enthusiastically. As children move up through the elementary grades, they take satisfaction in their research into an increasingly wide range of topics that provide real contexts in which to apply their expanding range of academic skills and knowledge.

Over several decades, we have worked with many teachers whose experience had been mainly whole group activity or whole class instruction. These teachers have reported their amazement and delight at how eagerly most children make choices, show initiative, contribute to group efforts, and respond to adult suggestions when working on a project. We recommend that the project approach be incorporated into the early childhood and elementary curriculum in the service of the major aims outlined in the following.

Intellectual Goals and the Life of the Mind: A Balance of Learning Experiences

In North America and in many other parts of the world, the curriculum of most education, even in the early years, increasingly places strong emphasis on academic goals, in particular the acquisition of basic academic skills. This trend toward early academic emphasis has been accompanied by widespread adoption of standards and tests at all age levels (Kendall, 2011).

An academic curriculum is typically organized in lock-step fashion so that all children pass through the same instructional sequences at about the same ages. The traditional three Rs that dominate an academic curriculum are also typically broken into discrete "skill and drill" sequences. The children are formally instructed in small or in large groups. They practice the skills by means of separate subtasks in workbooks and on work sheets. The content of these exercises is often unrelated to the world in which the children live and learn. Largely mindless, these activities usually mean little to the children, though at the outset, they are typically quite willing to learn with them.

A curriculum oriented toward academic goals puts a high priority on the needs, demands, and constraints of the academy itself and upon acquiring the narrow range of skills and dispositions required to function within it. In such a curriculum, the activities and content have more vertical—that is, future—usefulness than horizontal, or current, relevance.

Another basis for supporting the incorporation of project work into the early and elementary curriculum is that it puts a high priority on *intellectual* goals and ways of supporting them. The formal definition of the concept of "intellect" emphasizes reasoning, hypothesizing, predicting, developing and analyzing ideas, and the quest for fuller or deeper understandings of relevant phenomena. As already suggested, we propose here that children's minds are engaged in ways that deepen their understanding of their own experiences and environment. As they grow older, they can deepen their awareness and knowledge of others' experiences and environments and gradually strengthen their confidence in their own intellectual powers, as well as the practical *usefulness* of academic skills in their pursuit of knowledge. In other words, project work provides contexts in which children use their developing academic skills *in the service of their intellectual endeavors* (See also Nisbett, et al. 2012). While intellectual dispositions may be weakened by excessive premature academic instruction, they are also not likely to be strengthened by many of the trivial, if not banal, activities frequently offered in child care, preschool, kindergarten, and early primary classes.

Many educators, parents, and other adults tend to overestimate young children's academic readiness but to underestimate their intellectual abilities and dispositions. The extent to which young children's intellectual powers have traditionally been underestimated has become even clearer in recent years by the impressive work of the children in the preprimary schools in the northern Italian city of Reggio Emilia (Edwards, Gandini, and Forman, 1998; Katz & Cesarone, 1994). The careful and detailed documentation of the children's experiences, conversations, arguments, discussions, theories, and hypotheses provide compelling evidence of the intellectual powers of very young children and how they can be supported and strengthened in the course of good project work.

Careful documentation of the work of older children can also serve to deepen our awareness and appreciation of their growing capacities for intellectual pursuits. Our experience of working with teachers of elementary grade children confirms strongly their abilities and eagerness to engage in a wide range of intellectual processes: predicting events, hypothesizing their causes, theorizing about what might or could happen under various conditions, and many other intellectually based aspects of project work.

One example of such work is that of a class of mixed kindergarten and first-grade children who completed an extended, in-depth study of a nearby bicycle shop. They then created a bike shop in their own classroom. The teacher encouraged the children to develop many questions to put to those who worked in the bike shop when they visited it. Their questions ranged from matters of what could go wrong with a bicycle to its wheels and brakes and other parts, and they became deeply interested in how gears "mesh" on some of the bikes. The more they observed, the more questions and possible answers to them they created. Their minds were deeply engaged in the wide range of related topics for several months.

The minds of the children described at the beginning of this chapter were engaged in finding out about the parts of their school bus, their functions, and the safety provisions, and many of its other parts and how they work. The children had the chance to learn that everyday things can be full of interesting features to be studied in detail. Older children similarly can investigate complex machinery, nearby businesses, community activities, farming, etc. The high priority we give to the goal of intellectual involvement throughout the early and elementary school years is related to our commitment to four major and equally important goals of all education:

(1) The acquisition of knowledge and understanding,
(2) the acquisition and mastery of skills,
(3) the strengthening of important intellectual and social dispositions, and
(4) the development and management of important feelings. (See Katz, "Distinctions between Academic versus Intellectual Goals for Young Children." *NYSAEC Reporter* 39(2) (Winter 2012): 1–15.)

Balancing the Various Activities of the Children

We are not suggesting that project work, at any age level, should replace all current early childhood or primary school curriculum and practices. Rather, as a significant portion of the curriculum, project work can stimulate and strengthen the motivation to achieve mastery of their emerging skills, and it provides contexts in which the skills are applied purposefully. Teachers have frequently reported to us that in the processes of finding answers to their questions, children ask them for help in measuring, counting, subtracting, reading and writing complex texts, making Venn diagrams, and so forth—all in order to be able to document their findings that will answer the main question of their project investigation.

Wanerman (2013) makes a clear case for the value of project-type activities for toddlers. For preschool children, project work also supports coherence and continuity of their work together. It is that part of the curriculum in which the teacher intentionally guides and supports them in a variety of ways. In this sense, for preschoolers, a project is the relatively *more* teacher-directed part of the curriculum versus, for example, spontaneous play. However, because a project is emergent and negotiated rather than totally pre-planned by the teacher in the primary and elementary school years, it constitutes the *less* teacher-directed, more informal part of the curriculum compared to the formal instruction usually incorporated into the curriculum of the elementary and upper grades.

Many teachers of all age groups are under increasing pressure to meet their local, state, and national standards that constitute the bases of examinations, tests, and outcome measurements. Teachers of older children, and many of their parents as well, tend to emphasize academic instruction at the expense of the more spontaneous and creative aspects of the curriculum. Nevertheless, for most preschoolers, whole-class formal instruction in academic skills cannot be justified on the basis of available evidence of its long-term effects (Marcon, 2002).

As children grow, their capacities to benefit from formal academic instruction increases. From the age of about five years, many children can be profitably engaged in some formal small-group instruction in basic academic skills. As already suggested, the knowledge and skills acquired by formal instruction are likely to be strengthened by being applied and by serving purposes that are clear to the children. It is a good idea to keep in mind that skillfulness improves with *use* and not just instruction and isolated exercises. This implies that a curriculum is best when it includes systematic instruction and is balanced with the kind of project work described in the chapters that follow.

Building a Learning Community in the Class

Another aim of the project approach is to enable children to experience the class as a community. A community ethos is created when all of the children are expected and encouraged to contribute to the life of the whole group, even though they may do so in many different ways. Stevahn et al. (1996) point out that competitive environments are those in which individuals have a vested interest in others' failures; each works against the other "to achieve a goal that only one or a few can attain" (p. 803; See also Yeager & Dweck, 2012). In a similar way, individualistic environments are those in which individuals work independently of each other to achieve their own personal goals. In both competitive and individualistic contexts, participants tend to be dominated by short-term self-interests. In cooperative settings, on the other hand, individuals work together to achieve shared goals; their efforts are stimulated and supported by relatively long-term, mutual interests so that they strive to maximize joint outcomes. Project work provides ample opportunity for such a community with a cooperative ethos to flourish.

The children who studied their school bus, for example, shared a set of experiences they had in common. Studying different aspects of the topic of the bus in small groups and then sharing their groups' findings with each other strengthened their sense of belonging to a community of young investigators and scholars. Each child could appreciate the contribution of his or her own work to the resulting collective understanding developed by the whole class, encompassing a range of abilities, experiences, developmental levels, and backgrounds. This commitment to a community ethos in the class encourages us to provide contexts in which children work together, resolve their differences, accept different individual responsibilities, and contribute to the accomplishments of the whole class in differentiated ways.

Teachers play a major role in supporting the children's developing sense of belonging to the group and in helping them develop the many skills and insights involved in participating in and contributing to the community's group life. A wide range of skills, dispositions, and feelings are experienced and learned when the class works as a lively community doing together what they could not accomplish nearly so well individually or alone—these are life skills, dispositions, and feelings that are not included on standardized tests.

Education for Democracy

We suggest that another major aim served by the inclusion of project work in the curriculum is to help children to learn how to participate competently in a democratic society. This fundamental commitment to democracy means that opportunities are provided for children to investigate events and phenomena around them so that (a) they deepen their appreciation of the knowledge, skills, expertise, and efforts of others who contribute to their well-being in a wide variety of ways, (b) begin to learn the details of the ways in which members of a community are inter-dependent, and (c) learn to prize differences within their communities and perceive them as enriching.

Furthermore, democratic societies are most likely to flourish when their citizens seek in-depth understanding of the complex issues they must address and about which they must make decisions and choices. As already indicated, it is our view that project work provides contexts in which children's dispositions to seek in-depth understanding can be strengthened. In principle, unless children have experience of what it feels like to understand some things in increasing depth, they cannot develop the disposition to seek in-depth understanding and to pursue solutions to problems—both life-long dispositions we recommend.

Similarly, project work can strengthen children's dispositions to be empirical, that is, to seek and to examine available evidence and facts, checking their predictions and hypotheses, as well as to learn to be open to alternative ways of interpreting facts and findings. In addition, project work provides opportunities to strengthen the disposition to work hard; it presents occasions of having to do some things over again to meet the participants' developing standards and to find satisfaction in overcoming obstacles and difficulties. All of these are ways that the project approach contributes to children's early experience of aspects of democratic living. Many of the teachers we have worked with have indicated the extent to which they now realize they had previously underestimated children's capacities to gain satisfaction from hard work, cooperative efforts, and from overcoming the obstacles some of their work entailed.

The Challenges of Project Work for Teachers

Another aim of the project approach is for teachers themselves to experience their work as engaging and challenging. We have worked with teachers in many countries who work in a wide variety of situations and under diverse conditions. Some teachers must cope with poor physical facilities and limited supplies of learning materials. Still other teachers have very large classes and poor staff-child ratios. Many teachers of young children, especially the preschool and kindergartners, work with two different groups of children per day. Some teachers have one group on Mondays, Wednesdays, and Fridays, and another group on the other two weekdays. Thus, both groups must share the space and equipment in the classroom. Although these realities frequently present severe problems and frustrations, we have tried to emphasize that they can often be seen as challenges. The two examples below may be helpful.

The teacher of a morning group of four-year-olds was reluctant to undertake project work because she feared that the morning and the afternoon groups using the same room would spoil each other's work. Once she saw this difficulty as a challenge, however, she used it as an opportunity to help children learn to communicate with others. The morning group dictated a message to her to read to the afternoon group, saying, "We are building a police station in our classroom. Have you got some ideas?" The teacher read the message to her afternoon group, solicited their replies, and wrote them down. In the morning, the teacher read the afternoon group's message to the children, and they discussed its contents and offered comments and suggestions for the teacher to relay to the builders. The children in the morning group were able to carry on their project, which the afternoon children regularly inspected and commented on without interfering with the work. Both groups learned something about transmitting information to people who are not seen, and they gained some fresh understanding of the function and value of written communications.

The second example is that of a second-grade teacher who arrived at school one morning to find that a group of workers had started to repair the roof of her temporary classroom building. Neither she nor the principal had been forewarned, and no alternative classroom was available at the time. After a brief discussion with the principal about possible courses of action, she decided to stay in the classroom and organize the children in groups to conduct a day-long study of the whole event—in effect, to do a mini-project. Some of the children, working in pairs, accepted the responsibility of observing the workers' progress throughout the day. Other children accepted the assignment to interview the men about their tools, the materials, and the processes involved. Some of the children made a scale model of the classroom, roof and all, based on their measurements. Others drew the tools they observed, learned their names, and painted pictures of various aspects of the work. One of the workers was invited to talk to the class about roof repairs. The children studied the tools, different layers of roofing felt, and the tar or pitch, which had to be heated to specific temperatures. By the end of the day and on into the next day, the children created a wall display depicting and describing the event in rich detail (See also "Projects to Go" http://ceep.crc.illinois.edu/pubs.html).

In these two examples, creative and constructive solutions were found in response to problematic situations. On reflection, each teacher saw the situation in a positive light, accepting it as a challenge, rather than as a constraint on what could be accomplished. Creative solutions to the predicaments of teaching are not always possible. However, to respond to problems and constraints as challenges is a disposition worth cultivating in ourselves as well as in the children. The responses of the teachers in our examples were successful in part because they had respect for the children's potential abilities to take on the challenges with them.

A curriculum that limits the teacher primarily to daily formal instructional lessons and using the same texts and exercise books daily or weekly or to setting out the same toys and equipment for young children day after day can make teaching dreary and devoid of intellectual challenge. Many teachers have reported to us how their support and guidance of children conducting extensive, indepth investigation projects engaged their own minds and hearts more fully than did the traditional, formal, daily routines of teaching.

PROJECT WORK AND OTHER PARTS OF THE CURRICULUM

As already noted, we do not suggest that teachers discard all of their current practices and replace all of them with project work. We do recommend, however, that teachers experiment with project work in their present curriculum context and adapt it to their own aims and philosophies. Project work can thus complement and enhance what children learn through other parts of their curriculum.

In preschool, kindergarten, and elementary level settings, projects are among many other available activities. Appropriate materials and opportunities for spontaneous indoor and outdoor play, story reading, music, and other features of the typical early years curriculum continue alongside project work. As already indicated, the work of a project differs from the other parts of the early years and elementary curriculum in that it is based on the plans and intentions of individuals and/or groups, typically in consultation with their teacher. Preschool activities such as block-building, water play, and spontaneous dramatic play are usually activities that do not focus on a topic or involve detailed planning in advance or sustained effort over a period of days or weeks.

THE AGES OF THE CHILDREN

We address the project approach for a relatively wide age range—toddlers, preschoolers, and throughout the remaining levels of education. Those who study and work with children in this wide age range usually see it as a period in which intellectual development progresses at a rapid rate, especially during the first decade of life (See Wanerman, 2013). Although continuous, development is often uneven and sometimes progresses in spurts and does linger occasionally on plateaus. Furthermore, child development is typically idiosyncratic, varying with the individual characteristics, circumstances, and experiences of the child. First, the project approach takes into account the unevenness of development by enabling children to undertake open-ended tasks alongside one another at varying levels of complexity and with equally acceptable alternative outcomes. Consider, for example, a project in which five-year-olds investigate the distance that different balls will roll freely along the floor after rolling down an inclined plane they created placing a plank against a pile of blocks. One child is just able to release the balls, while another has the knowledge and skills needed to note and write down the measure of the distance the balls had rolled. Both children participate and contribute to the completion of the task, but at quite different levels. It is a good idea to assume that age itself is at best a rough predictor of children's capabilities.

Second, the project approach lends itself particularly well to teaching children of different ages within a class or setting. In many early childhood settings around the world, teachers work with groups mixed in age as well as in ability. The project approach is particularly suited to capitalizing on the differences among the children in mixed age groups. Among the many advantages of project work in mixed age groups (Katz, Evangelou, & Hartmann, 1990) is that the younger ones are more likely to be included in the work and challenged by the work that has been initiated by the older children among them than would be possible if they were in an age-segregated class.

Third, we especially want to emphasize how the same topics can be fruitfully studied by children from age four to eight or ten years of age in accordance with their developing intellectual, academic, and social competencies. As children's knowledge and skills accumulate and develop, the work grows in depth, complexity, and sophistication. Thus, for example, kindergarten teachers need not be concerned if their pupils had already studied the weather in their preschool classes. Throughout childhood, projects on most topics can be undertaken in such a way that knowledge and understanding continue to deepen and become more differentiated and complex.

In the project work described in the chapters that follow, we suggest that children of varying ages and abilities work together, contributing to the group effort, studying the same topic continuously, extending and deepening their knowledge of it, and increasing the skillfulness with which they work.

NOTE

1. See, for example, a brief summary of an in-depth investigation of water conducted by children in three parallel classes age range 3- to 7-years-old. Accessible at: <:http://education.illinois.edu/news/ UPS-students-culminate-semester-long-study-water-displaying-models-and-other-modes-learning>.

TWO

Phases and Features of a Project and Teacher Planning

Projects can be short-term undertakings, or they might enliven a classroom for eight weeks or longer. Short-term, small-group, or spontaneously generated projects that we refer to as mini-projects require little advanced teacher planning. Occasionally a mini-project arises at the beginning or end of the school year or from an unexpected event, such as the resurfacing of the schoolyard or bees swarming nearby. In such cases, advanced planning is not possible. However, if a project is to last several weeks and involve the whole class, advanced planning improves the chances of fruitful investigation and accomplishment. This chapter describes some techniques for initial project planning and suggests ways to elaborate plans and adapt topics for particular groups of children.

We begin the discussion of planning with reference to a time-scale for projects and the characterization of the early, middle, and later phases in the course of a project. We then describe five features that function across all three phases to facilitate the planning, guidance, and evaluation of the project as it develops. These five features are (a) discussion, (b) field work, (c) investigation, (d) representation, and (e) display. The later section of the chapter concerns the role of the teacher in developing the project topic as well as creating and managing the learning environment of the classroom. This chapter concludes with a discussion of the benefits to the learner of opportunities to exercise genuine choice. The structure underlying the implementation of the project approach is one that enables the teacher to be flexible and responsive to children's interests and learning needs while continuing to exercise leadership in facilitating work of a high quality for all participating children.

PHASES OF PROJECT WORK

Projects can be described as having three general phases that typically merge into each other. This temporal framework is designed to help teachers systematically focus children's attention on the topic of study. It is similar to the structure of a good story, having a beginning, a middle, and an end. This framework can help projects to develop with a narrative quality, making them optimally productive and memorable. Outlined briefly below, each phase is explicated more fully in later chapters.

Phase I: Planning and Getting Started

A project can begin in several ways. Some begin when one or more of the children in a group express an interest in something that attracts their attention. Some projects begin when the teacher introduces a topic or when a topic is selected by agreement between the teacher and the children. Often this is done with an initial provocation, a small-scale display of materials or objects that invite discussion among the children. In the upper elementary years, it may be that a project topic is suggested by the social studies or science curriculum. In many cases, projects provide a link between different subjects that would otherwise be taught in separate lessons. One grade 5 class (10–11-year-olds) undertook a project on the nearby river in which they engaged in a good deal of mapping as well as learning about environmental science and health issues as they studied the rivers within their state.

The main thrust of the first phase of project work is to establish common ground among the participating children by enabling them to share the information, ideas, and experiences they already have about the topic. At this time the teacher can help the children to build a common basic understanding from which to begin their investigation of the topic in more detail. For instance, in the school bus project, the young children discussed their experiences, noting those that were common to them all: waiting for the bus, climbing aboard, finding a seat, riding through the town, and getting off at the school. They also shared less common experiences, such as being the first or the last to board the bus, just missing the bus and having to get to school some other way, the bus driver arguing with a policeman, and being on the bus the morning it broke down.

During preliminary discussions, the teacher encourages the children to talk about the topic, to play, and to depict their current understandings of it in other ways. The teacher takes the opportunity to serve as a source of advice and suggestions. Parents can be informed of the topic of study and invited to participate in any way they can in the project. Children are invited to bring pertinent objects from home and collect materials for the construction activities of the project. In the case of older students, the first phase may take less time and involve fewer practical activities as they share their initial understandings.

The exchange of personal experiences gives rise to an appreciation of both common and more idiosyncratic experiences children have had related to the topic. It also helps the teacher to learn which children know a great deal already about the topic and which children have only limited experience. Sometimes children with similar experiences have very different ways of understanding those experiences. Teachers can probe stories of experience, inviting children to reveal their understandings. A focus on explanation offers children opportunities to wonder about how things come about and the reasons things happen the way they sometimes do. Such wondering on the children's part helps them to learn more about cause and effect relations and to think of questions and to consider ways to find out more than they currently know.

Discussions in the first phase of the project on pets, for instance, might suggest many aspects of the topic to wonder about. Why do some people decide to keep snakes or cats or guinea pigs? How much does it cost to keep different kinds of pets? Where do different kinds of pets sleep? and so on. Many children are very willing to suggest various opinions on these matters, and the differences among them can help the teacher to formulate questions with the children so that their later research can yield pertinent information.

The children and teacher can develop plans for conducting investigations, make arrangements for visits or visitors, and develop a variety of initial questions to be answered by the investigations. Procedures for obtaining construction materials are also worked out at this time. Some preliminary investigations upon which to build later ones might also be introduced during this phase. For example, a project about clothes might begin by taking a close look at the children's coats and noting colors, types of buttons, belts, and fabrics. Later investigations would make use of this background understanding of the different parts of coats to investigate how they are made.

Throughout the first phase, the teacher can help younger children develop the vocabulary necessary for discussion of the topic. Older students can develop topic webs together in groups or individually to sort the vocabulary into subtopics. This collection of vocabulary helps the teacher to map out the scope of the topic in discussion with the students and can allow for additional technical terms to be added as the project progresses. It also provides the students with a useful resource to refer to for spelling or more information.

Phase II: Projects in Progress

During the second phase of a project, the main emphasis of the teacher's work is on enabling the children to acquire new information. The teacher arranges visits outside the school, invites visitors to talk to the children or demonstrate special expertise, and collects real objects, books, photographs, or artifacts for the children to study in the classroom. For example, a group (or a whole class) of children studying shopping might visit nearby stores. The visit may include talking to storekeepers and buying some items to take back to the classroom. This shared event provides a common background of experience on which to negotiate new understandings. The visit can enhance the realism with which the children play "stores" and "shopping" in the classroom. Visits also increase the likelihood that the children will ask for clarification of their perceptions of what they have experienced together.

In a hospital project, the teacher might arrange for a nurse or a doctor to talk with the children and leave them some spare instruments or X-rays as props for their play. The children could explore the new sources of information, assimilate the new knowledge, and identify and revise misconceptions through interaction with their classmates and the teacher.

In the second phase of a project— about going to school on the bus, for example, the teacher might arrange for a detailed study of the bus itself and ask that it be brought to school earlier than usual so that the children can talk to the driver and inspect the different parts of the vehicle. They might build a bus in the classroom or draw, paint, and write about the bus, its journeys to school, traffic regulations, the role of the police, the different modes of transport by which the children come to school, the distances and times that different children travel. The second phase, along with the first, gives children common script knowledge (knowledge about sequences of events that invariably form part of a process [Nelson, 1986]): waiting for the bus, climbing aboard, remaining seated, wearing a seat belt, etc.—all familiar aspects of going to school on the bus. They also learn about less common occurrences, dangers, and emergencies, as well as normal experiences and safety precautions.

An important role of the teacher during this second phase is to encourage children's independent use of the skills they already have. These skills include observation, communication, drawing, and painting. Older children can apply their developing competence in writing, reading, calculating, and doing research. In this phase, the teacher can also attend to strengthening the children's dispositions to pursue and find out more about a topic that interests them. The teacher provides materials and offers suggestions and advice about appropriate ways to represent their findings and ideas.

Phase III: Reflections and Conclusions

The main thrust of the third phase of project work is to help bring the project to completion with group and individual work and to summarize what has been learned. In the third phase, it is hoped that most of the children will share a thorough understanding of the topic. Introducing new information at this time may be inadvisable. Instead, what is required is an elaboration of the children's learning so that its meaning is enhanced and made personal. We assume that as children apply their new knowledge, they can make it truly their own.

For the older children, the third phase of a project is a time of rehearsal and reflection on the new levels of understanding and knowledge acquired. They express their increased knowledge not only in play but also in wall displays, music, drama and dance, making class books, games, and folders of individual work. Sometimes a culminating activity can be organized so that children can present what they have learned to their classmates. They may invite their parents or children from other classes to see their work and explain what they have learned, how they learned it, and the procedures they used to develop the project.

For three- and four-year-olds, the third phase is usually a time for them to role-play in their project constructions. Thus, if they have built a doctor's office or a shop, this phase will consist mainly of enacting the various roles they associate with those settings. The social and dramatic play helps them to integrate their modified and fuller understanding of the real world.

In the third phase of the school bus project, the teacher can help children to elaborate their play with the bus they constructed. The class can discuss possible school bus stories for dramatic play: a story or play about the day the school bus had to go a different way because a tree had fallen across the road in a storm, or the day the children helped the driver change a flat tire. They can also dictate or write their stories. They can play or make up games, such as dice and board games, in which the progress of the bus is hindered or facilitated along the way to school. They can make up new songs and poems about the bus if they have not done so already. They can make a pictorial story that illustrates the journey to school. Older students might share their work through setting up a museum or a restaurant or putting on a performance, which they direct themselves.

The Three Phases Illustrated in Dramatic Play

In dramatic play in the context of a project, children negotiate and refine their growing understanding of their topic by consulting with other children and the teacher. For example, in the first phase of the hospital project, prior understandings are expressed and shared in play. Early in the project, children might role-play their experiences of visits to the doctor, being ill at home, or patching up a grazed knee.

In Phase II, new information is tried out. The teacher may have read the children a story about a girl who broke her arm and had to go to the hospital, have it set in a plaster cast, and have the cast removed. The children might try out their newly acquired script information by acting out a visit to the hospital to have an injured arm X-rayed, followed by the succession of events as described in the story.

In Phase III, children consolidate new understandings. During the dramatic play of the third phase of a hospital project, the children may be happy to play various combinations of events: accidents involving broken bones, visits to the doctor's office and to the hospital to see the specialist, being X-rayed, and having plaster casts put on and removed. In this more extended and elaborate play, old understandings are clarified and enriched by newly acquired script knowledge.

FIVE FEATURES OF PROJECT WORK

When the project approach is done well, there is evidence of judicious structuring of the project by the teacher. Successful projects have a flexible framework made up of several features that apply across the three phases in the life of a project. In this section of the chapter, we describe five features in particular that enable teachers to develop projects that respond to children's interests and learning needs: discussion, field work, representation, investigation, and display. These features can help children become highly motivated, feel actively engaged in their learning, and produce work of a high quality.

Discussion

Discussion can take place during a whole class meeting, among a small group of children, or between two children. Discussion can be engaged in by children with the teacher or other adult, teacher's aide, parent volunteer, or visiting expert to the classroom. Many discussions may also be part of children's collaborative activity without the direct involvement of the teacher.

Discussion in the context of a project is different from the kind of whole group teacher interaction that often takes place, for example, in the context of direct instruction. Discussion in a project involves children talking to each other and not referring back to the teacher between each child's contribution. Children learn to talk to each other, to question each other, to comment on each other's ideas, and to request clarification or additional information from other children, as well as from the teacher. This kind of discussion is well described by Gallas as "what happens to talk when children are encouraged to speak collaboratively and develop ideas from their own life experience" (1994, 84). Discussion has several important functions for adults and children in a project. Five of these will be mentioned here.

First, discussion is a way of exchanging information about the topic of study. As children increase their knowledge about the topic, they can share their discoveries with their peers. In this way, they are able to review what they have learned by explaining it to their classmates for the agreed purpose of making sure that everyone is informed about what is being learned by others. Second, the children can discuss the strategies they are engaged in for investigation and representation in the context of the project. Discussion of these strategies helps all children in their work, reminding them of the range of different ways they can learn. Third, discussion provides children with opportunities to solicit suggestions from peers of how to improve a piece of work or solve a problem. This function of discussion allows children to learn from the work of other children and develop confidence in the availability of different kinds of help they can seek in the classroom. Fourth, discussion provides a context within which children can demonstrate their growing understanding to the teacher. Fifth, the children can be involved with the teacher in planning the development of the project as the study progresses. They can do this in reference to a topic web, which the teacher can develop with them throughout the project. In the first phase, the topic web can begin with vocabulary collected from the children's own stories of experience, their questions, and their predictions of possible answers. Later, additional vocabulary is added to the web to allow for the children's vocabulary to grow more detailed and provide for a more accurate understanding of the topic through their investigation of it.

Field Work

The study of real world topics where there is local expertise available offers great advantages to the teacher. The children can learn from many sources of information, such as visits to local field sites and interviews with local experts. It is also helpful to see how many of the children's families have access to relevant expertise through training, experience, interest, or travel.

"Field work" might be defined as any activity which takes place outside the classroom. In the first phase of a project, children might interview their parents about experiences they have had relevant to the topic. In the second phase, the teacher can take children out into the community where there are relevant objects, vehicles, machines, people, events, and processes to observe first hand. Children are ideally suited to learning from complex reality, as is shown by the ease with which they learn a new language when they hear it spoken all around them. Individuals in a class of children notice different details at a field site. Depending on their ages, the children in a class can become quite efficient at recording these observations in field notes, a genre of representation which may combine drawing, writing, numbers, and simple diagrams. A rich pool of information can result from one field visit when the teacher can find ways to collect, sort, discuss, and make available the children's observations.

Representation

Children can represent their experience, prior knowledge, questions, research findings, and explanations in a variety of ways through dramatic play, drawing, construction, writing, and designing graphic organizers. From the beginning of any project, the teacher can help children share experiences, knowledge, and skills with one another through selected representations, drawing, painting, model making, writing, maps, etc. Children can also combine representational strategies to clarify and elaborate the information they plan to share. Pictures can be presented with captions, diagrams with descriptions of what they represent, and so on. As children grow older, they acquire a wider range of representational strategies. In the context of a project, different children might at any one time be using a variety of such strategies. Through the discussion of the work being done, all participating children are frequently reminded of the range of representational strategies open to them in their work.

Investigation

Projects always involve some kind of research. Much research can be first hand, and findings are gained from close observation and interviewing experts. There is also an increasing emphasis as children become older on secondary source research: finding out information from books, videos, museum exhibits, and other sources where information has been prepared and presented by other researchers. In the elementary school, textbooks are sometimes superseded by newer ones or are abandoned for different learning material. Older textbooks could still be made available for research by individual children where appropriate.

First hand research can be carried out through field work. In classrooms, it can also take the form of explorations or experiments with material, objects, or substances. Small animals or insects can be studied first hand in classrooms with the proviso that due care is taken to treat live material in an ethically responsible way.

Display

Display is one of the important aspects of documentation. The story of the project is built up visually as the work of the children is displayed in the classroom. The teacher can use bulletin boards, classroom walls, shelves, and table surfaces to display information, children's work, collections of objects, lists of words, books to consult, instructions for procedures, and materials and equipment to work with. These displays provide children with the

Table 2.1 Overview of Phases and Structural Features

	Discussion	Fieldwork	Representation	Investigation	Display
Phase 1 beginning the project	• Sharing prior experience and current knowledge of a topic	• Children talking about their prior experience with their parents and caregivers	• Using drawing, writing, construction, and dramatic play to share prior experience and knowledge	• Raising questions on the basis of current knowledge	• Sharing representation
Phase 2 developing the project	• Preparing for fieldwork and interviews • Reviewing fieldwork • Learning from secondary sources	• Going out of the classroom to investigate a field site • Interviewing experts in the field or in the classroom	• Brief field sketches and notes • Using drawing, painting, writing, math, diagrams, and maps to represent new learning	• Investigating initial questions • Fieldwork and library research • Raising further questions	• Sharing representations of new experience and knowledge • Keeping ongoing records of the project work
Phase 3 concluding the project	• Preparing to share the story of the project • Reviewing and evaluating the project	• Evaluating the project through the eyes of an outside group	• Considering and summarizing the story of the study to share the project with others	• Speculating about new questions	• Summary of the learning throughout the project

Source: Sylvia E. Chard. Practical Guide 2. The Project Approach to Managing Successful Projects.

documentation of processes and products of the project. Seeing examples of project work posted in the classroom allows them to become more familiar with both the information they represent and with the means used to share that information.

Teachers who have experience working this way value opportunities to observe and interact with children involved in dramatic play or to help with construction techniques. This approach also enables the teacher to move around the classroom for much of the time and support the children in whatever they are doing. The teacher can use the time to encourage their efforts and, where appropriate, to suggest ideas. In project work, the teacher's role is more that of adviser and guide than an instructor.

Over the course of a project, the teacher can help children appreciate the ways their work is developing. The teacher collects and displays work products, presenting the progress of groups and individuals to the whole class by means of discussion and display. There can be ongoing evaluation as different items are selected for display on the walls of the classroom. In the first phase, the teacher can display the representations of children's prior experience and knowledge. These representations may include the following: results of surveys, bar charts of the experiences of groups or of the whole class (e.g. grocery shopping, pet ownership, grand-parents living locally), comparisons of one child's experience with another (e.g., travelling on a ferry or going fishing), drawings with captions or written descriptions with picture illustrations (accounts of personal experience), reports of interviews (one child with another, where one child explains his or her experience to another child who has not had the same experience), etc. In the second phase of a project, the children's work consists of field notes, reports of investigations and the findings of these, and representations of growing understanding in written reports, murals, graphs, maps, timelines, and other graphic organizers, as well as through computer technology.

DEVELOPING THE STUDY OF THE TOPIC WITH CHILDREN

As indicated in the discussion of issues in topic selection in chapter 3, the choice of topics for projects may be made in a variety of

Figure 2.1   Teacher's web of the topic of the construction site

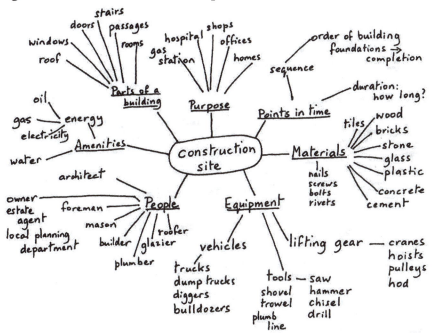

ways according to the practices and preferences of the school. Individual teachers may independently select topics for their classes, or schools may develop a policy of offering specific major projects in each grade each year. In the elementary years, teachers develop some projects on the basis of a social studies or science curriculum guide required by the school authorities. Sometimes a whole school undertakes one project. In such cases, teachers plan as a team, and each class takes responsibility for a particular area or subtopic related to the main one. Occasionally, the children in a class select a topic and the teacher helps develop and refine its scope in discussion with them.

Once a suitable topic has been selected, the teacher sets out some provisional plans on paper. One technique teachers have adapted for this purpose is that of creating what we call a "topic web." This is a diagram in which ideas and information are grouped under subtopic headings. A major advantage of a topic web is that the ideas can be generated in any order; no predetermined sequence is dictated by the form of the web. In that respect, it is different from a flow chart, which has a linear temporal sequence built into it.

The Teacher's Topic Web

A web is a graphic mapping of the key ideas and concepts that a topic comprises and some of the major subtopics related to it. Teachers could, of course, work with a web designed by someone else. But the process of making a web in and of itself often helps teachers to become aware of their own knowledge and resources. Some teachers inexperienced in the project approach have reported to us that brainstorming a topic web increased their awareness of how much they did or did not know about a topic before they began searching information in a reference work. Teachers often report a tendency to underestimate their own knowledge of a topic as well as how much young children can learn from real objects, people, and places, as well as from books. It is generally helpful at first for the teacher to consider more ideas than could possibly be used in a single project. In the first place, not all of the ideas generated by brainstorming will be suitable as areas of investigation by the children. Second, if a teacher has considered a wide range of possibilities by him or herself, it will be easier later on to incorporate the ideas that children may offer in a preliminary discussion.

Linking Project Topics to Curriculum Areas

When the web is completed, it is useful to produce a second web that organizes the project ideas under curriculum subject area headings and the learning activities associated with them according to the age of the children in the class. Keep in mind, however, that the curriculum subject web should be developed only *after* the first kind of brainstorming has been completed. This sequence minimizes the likelihood of distorting the topic itself toward setting tasks within conventional curriculum subject boundaries.

Appropriate learning goals for children are more likely to be addressed by using the "brainstorming" web that reflects relationships among the items of information about the topic itself. The curriculum subject web, on the other hand, reflects the teacher's purposes, which may or may not correspond with the web developed later with the children. For example, measuring the size of a vehicle involves exercising considerable mathematical skill. However, if the vehicle is measured only because the teacher wants the children to practice measurement, then it will be of less value as a project activity than if the children do so in the course of planning to make a model of a vehicle to scale. Making a model to understand how the vehicle works provides opportunities for practicing measurement skills, rather than the other way around.

Deciding on the Scope of a Project

The more general and abstract a topic, the more scope it has for subdividing the content. With each subdivision, topics become smaller until they are relatively microscopic. In the reverse direction, larger topics can be created by combining small, related topics. We suggest here that smaller and more specific topics are probably more suitable for younger children. As children get older, they can more easily see connections between subtopics within larger topics with a wider scope.

One technique for narrowing the topic involves focusing on just one or two subtopics in the web. The subtopic title(s) then become the center of a new web, which can be as elaborate as the previous one on the main topic. For example, in a hospital web, the ambulance can become a focus. At the center of a new web, the ambulance can have subtopics such as motor, wheels, emergency equipment, siren, flashing lights, materials, driver, emergencies, routes to the hospital, and shifts worked by the driver.

A second technique for narrowing or broadening the focus of a topic is to think in terms of its specificity or generality. Related topics can be located in a hierarchical classification, from the more specific to the more general. The more specific a topic, the more likely it is to be suitable for a project with younger children. Examples of hierarchically related topics that vary in scope are as follows:

1. hats, uniforms, period costume, clothes, the fashion industry

2. tortoises, reptiles, wild animals, zoology

3. my bedroom, my house, our village, our state, our country
4. weather, seasons, local climate, global climate change

The choice of project title as a focus for the work need not be limiting, however. In the case of the weather, no matter how young the children, the work can be extended to include the seasons or the climate. These more remote, abstract concepts would not be as fully developed by the younger ones as by older children.

A third way of narrowing the scope of a topic, especially for children in the preschool period, is to predicate it in some way, as Blank (1985) suggests. Blank argues that the predication of a concept is vital to any dialogue about it. It is difficult to have a conversation about food, for example, until the term is predicated in some way that gives it a particular contextual meaning. Once it is known whether one is thinking about buying food, serving food, or preparing food, the word "food" takes on a significance that can generate conversation. Giving alternative perspectives to the topic of houses can indicate a direction for study: "building a house," "houses in our neighborhood," or "furnishing a house." A project about shops may have subthemes, such as "going shopping," "shops in our Main Street," or "setting up a shop."

Predicates can be particularly useful in reflecting the children's interests and ideas on a main topic. The three techniques discussed here for narrowing the scope of a topic for a project with younger children or for completing it in a shorter time have been found useful by teachers in adapting topics for particular groups of children.

THE ROLE OF THE TEACHER

In project work, the teacher's role is more that of a guide than a director. It is the teacher's responsibility to set clear expectations for the quality of the work to be accomplished and for the children's conduct and, at the same time, to develop a classroom climate that facilitates the open exchange of information. As the children set to work on drawing, painting, writing, diagrams, etc., they need access to materials, tools, and appropriate places to work. In a well-organized classroom, the children come to know how best to get to work efficiently with what they need so as to minimize confusion or waste of time.

Procedures are very important in the project approach because children work individually and in small groups over periods of several days or weeks. Young children need frequent reminders about the alternative strategies open to them, about what they should be doing, and about where, when, and with whom they should be doing it. These reminders are not always stated in the form of instructions, however. Many are expressed as suggestions or options to be considered by specific groups or individuals. Other reminders can take the form of examples referring to individuals who worked in a particularly successful way, who chose carefully, and who can talk about the reasons for their decisions. Children do not usually recount their experiences to show off or to intimidate other children but to explain how they approached the problems they encountered. The older children's attention can often be drawn to the notices around the room, indicating what to do and how to set about doing it. Notices might be entitled: "Is your representation complete? Check this list. . ." or "Things to be finished before Thursday."

The teacher can use many devices to strengthen the children's dispositions to be resourceful and independent as they work on projects. For instance, the teacher can ensure that children have easy access to materials and equipment set out for them, that books and displays are readily available to be consulted for information, and that resources such as vocabulary lists are conveniently located in the classroom to help children with their writing. During class discussion, children can be reminded of the procedures for helping themselves and each other when the teacher's attention is taken up elsewhere.

In classrooms where projects are being developed, the free exchange of information contributes to the smooth running of the class. Here, the information emanates not only from the teacher but also from children's reports of their own understanding and the progress they are making. Children can help one another a great deal by example and as consultants and collaborators. Since much of this work represents information, it can be displayed to serve as a resource for other children while they pursue their investigations. The teacher also has an important role to play in helping children appreciate each other's work.

FIVE PLANNING CRITERIA

In chapter 3, we discuss *relevance* to the children's own experience as a principal criterion for selecting project topics. We also consider five other criteria for selecting and focusing particular project topics: the activities the children can undertake, applying skills, the availability of resources, the interest of the teacher, and the time of the school year.

Activities for the Children

No matter what the topic, certain kinds of worthwhile knowledge, skills, dispositions, and feelings can be developed through project work. Although groups of children may undertake projects on different topics, much similar learning will take place. Whether the children study "birds feeding," "vehicles for cargo," or "clothes for cold weather," each topic offers opportunities for close observation, labeling of parts, counting and tallying (counting in groups), making bar charts, sorting according to different criteria, finding and recording information from books, negotiating with other children, and collaborating in group activities. The activities give children the occasion to observe, to reconstruct aspects of the environment, and to practice finding things out. These skills and processes are being learned and applied with every project undertaken, although the prominence given to particular skills and processes may vary from one topic to another.

During initial planning, the teacher develops a web of relevant vocabulary with the children. A familiar hospital in the neighborhood can be an important focal point in the web and project plans. Some of the children might have had relatives there or have been hospital patients themselves. It is likely that they and their siblings were born in the hospital. Some of the parents might work there. If so, one part of the web may be developed more fully to include resources well known to the children.

Finding out what the children already know about hospitals might best be achieved by asking children to explore the common experiences they have had with local doctors. These experiences vary in different parts of the world. Children in rural areas of China are likely to be familiar with the barefoot doctor, her role in the community, and the instruments she uses. Children in rural India will probably be familiar with the primary health center in their community and its procedures and services. Many children in the Australian outback will have experience with visits from the flying doctor. Whatever the location, the doctor or district nurse might be willing to visit the school to talk to the children. Each culture offers different perspectives on the topic, and these can be reflected in the activities of the children as they develop the project.

Applying Skills

Project work gives children the opportunity to apply skills independently for purposes that they themselves have generated or helped to formulate. These purposes will arise from the children's own experiences. Even within one class, children show different levels of competence and confidence in a variety of basic skills. Most children apply skills independently only when they feel confident and comfortable enough in the classroom setting.

Sometimes confident children, highly motivated to obtain information from a reference book, persist with reading the material even though much of it is too difficult for them. Similarly, in adult life, people may choose at times to attempt difficult tasks that stretch them almost beyond the limits of their ability, and at other times, they may confidently prefer to work with more risk-taking and originality at something that is easy for them. So too in project work. Children can choose from a variety of levels of challenge. This is another example of the way project work can bring activities in school closer to the quality of real-life experience, a major theme of the project approach. Projects offer the teacher opportunities to encourage children to work at an optimum level of confidence and to select different levels of challenge.

When children work independently, they might be expected to take more time at their tasks, to take risks, to be more exploratory and imaginative in their thinking than under conditions of direct instruction. For example, preschool children can learn about the purposes of reading and writing before they can actually read or write. In their play, they can make shopping lists, "write" prescriptions, or follow recipes. Play or pretend writing may take the form of scribbling, even after children are receiving writing instruction, just as there is a short overlap between a baby's crawling and walking, when both methods of locomotion are practiced alternately. When writing comes to children easily, they use it with fluency and have no need for scribbling, just as infants drop the crawling when they become confident walkers.

The application of language skills is an important concern in teacher planning of projects. Project work provides rich content for conversation, not only on the topic itself, but also on the range of processes involved in the work, such as planning constructions, deciding on procedures and the materials to be used, and so forth. Project work offers children shared experiences of events to think about and discuss with one another. The experiences gained while working together on various aspects of the project become integrated with current understandings as children talk in a variety of situations. The dramatic play area (e.g. housekeeping corner, domestic play space) can be equipped with props that stimulate conversation in role-playing. When children not only dress up in nurses' and doctors' uniforms but also have a stethoscope, syringes (with needles removed, of course), a thermometer, a sling, bandages, a blood pressure gauge, and empty medicine bottles, their play becomes considerably more focused on specific information. They can think about the diagnosis and treatment of illness and what medical personnel can do to help. Thus, many aspects of language development are stimulated and strengthened in the contexts provided by project work. As they involve themselves in the activities of planning, checking, collaborating, and coordinating their efforts, children use language purposefully and gain satisfaction from their own sense of effectiveness.

Language is the principal means by which young children can share, negotiate, and even create meaning. In the process of planning, the teacher can assess the potential of the project for adding to the children's growing store of words, expressions, and phrases. Children not only have to acquire new vocabulary. They also have to learn ways of using the words associated with basic sequences of related events leading to predictable outcomes in particular contexts and for particular purposes. For example, eating out in a restaurant has the following sequence of: entering the restaurant, being seated at a table, looking at menus, choosing courses for a meal, ordering from a waiter, waiting for the meal to come to the table, eating the meal, paying for it, and leaving the restaurant.

While selecting and planning a suitable project, teachers can list the vocabulary, expressions, and concepts associated with different understandings. For example, "diagnosis" involves finding out what is wrong with a patient, where it hurts, how much it hurts, how hot she is, and how long she has been ill. "Treatment," on the other hand, refers to what must be done to help the person feel better and recover from the illness or injury. The two concepts, diagnosis and treatment, are distinct; though similar vocabulary is used, "diagnosis" and "treatment" are terms used to talk and think about matters associated with different purposes.

During planning, teachers can take into account the ways that children use their behavioral knowledge in developing their representational knowledge. When visiting the doctor, for example, children may exhibit the behavioral knowledge of being a patient: showing their tongue, coughing on request, and later taking medicine. The project activities help children develop representational knowledge that distinguishes behaviors related to diagnosis from those concerned with treatment.

Various cognitive processes are involved in the development of representational knowledge. Children actively engage in comparing and contrasting objects and events, note attributes of things, take them apart and reassemble them, group objects into classes, order them, and string them together in sequences. Appropriate communicative skills can be developed as children work cooperatively, questioning, speculating, reasoning, inferring, arguing about, and explaining their project-related work and actions. For the youngest children in the age range of concern here, communicative competence can be strengthened when they are encouraged to ask each other's advice, tell each other what they are planning to do, and ask each other questions about their work and progress in the project.

The basic academic skills of reading, writing, and mathematics can be employed when school-age children record observations, describe experiences, and note down what they have found out in books. Some projects offer greater opportunities than other projects for applying certain basic skills. In a store project with older children, there might be more opportunities for particular mathe-matical skills to be applied; in a study of the neighborhood, map reading and other graphic skills can be used. Most projects provide many varied opportunities for using skills in drawing, talking, writing, reading, mathematics, and science.

Some topics are particularly rich in potential for investigative ac-tivities, while others offer more opportunities for dramatic play. In their planning, teachers are generally concerned with achieving a long-term balance in the kinds of learning opportunities that the project is likely to provide for the children.

Accessing Resources

The term "resources" is used very broadly here to include any sources of information and experience, such as field trips and class-room visitors, as well as material resources that contribute to the activities and learning of the children. The resources available for the children's work and play are a major consideration for the teacher when planning a project.

If, for example, the teacher introduces a project on "going to the hospital," she might ask herself the following questions about resources: Where might the children visit (local clinic, doctor's office)? Who might be invited to talk to them in school (nurse, doc-tor)? Might this visitor have some discarded instruments, some old X-ray pictures to donate to the project? What resources does the school have from previous hospital projects (doctors' and nurses' coats and uniforms, charts, books)?

Teachers experienced in using the project approach often accu-mulate a personal collection of potentially useful items. In addition, parents may be requested to contribute to the school's collection by donating equipment and other items to exhibit, to work with, or to enrich play, for example, bandages, crutches, and empty medicine bottles.

Sources of information, experience, and resources can also be found beyond the school walls: the public library, local museum, businesses, factories, and educational resource centers. For exam-ple, children growing up in a fishing village can gain much knowl-edge from a project on "How do we get our fish?" or "Boats used for fishing." There is also a particular value in the children collecting resources from home, being given or loaned items, and collecting some on a visit they themselves have made. This initiative further illustrates the principle that young children's learning is maximized through effective interaction with their environment and the people in their community.

One of the most important aspects of good project work is that it is planned so as to include a significant proportion of firsthand and direct experience of real objects and people. The proportion of such experiences should be high in relation to secondhand information gained from books and visits to museums, where the information has already been experienced and presented by someone else.

If the project topic is about the neighborhood, local industry, or the surrounding natural environment, then resources may be plentiful and easy to obtain. Parents can be involved in the project, talking to the children about some special expertise, helping with field trips, and lending or giving objects, pictures, photographs, or other resources to the classroom. For topics that are distant in time (e.g., Victorian England or castles) or distant in space (e.g., Japan or animals in the Polar Regions), only secondhand and indirect information would be available to the children, causing them to be very dependent on the teacher for their thinking, planning, and learning. Projects of this type are not suitable because they provide little or no personal firsthand experience and firsthand information on which children can base their contributions to the work of the project.

When children are older (from eight to twelve years), they have enough general knowledge and awareness of learning strategies to learn a great deal from secondary sources. In the upper elementary school years, students can make increasingly complex inferences to understand information that is outside their own direct experience. They also come to understand a set of public concepts that approximate or overlap those of the adult culture.

For young children, however, the availability of a store of general knowledge cannot be relied upon because their knowledge of the larger world is still being formed. When, for example, nine-year-olds study the river Nile, some general knowledge about a local river can be relied upon. But young children acquire general knowledge about rivers most easily through studying a nearby river, one whose bridges they cross with their parents, fish in, or walk beside. The teacher can share the children's experience of the river on a field trip and gain a fuller insight into their interests and understanding.

Teacher Interest

It is also helpful if the teacher chooses a topic in which she herself has some personal interest and basic knowledge. In project work, the teacher is an important model to the children. She exemplifies the dispositions she wishes to strengthen by helping children with their explorations, by encouraging and acknowledging questions, discussing, and demonstrating an inquiring disposition. To do so, she uses books, pictures, charts, maps, and so forth to find out where the children can look for appropriate information.

Because the range of topics is wide, teachers need not repeat the same projects every year or even every three or four years. Each year, they can usually plan some projects that are new, fresh, and personally challenging to themselves as well as to the children. However, since the children have an important influence on the way projects develop, a responsive teacher seldom finds that even a repeated project takes the same course with a different class group.

One teacher of kindergarten children told us about a project on pets, which she had done every year for four years. In response to our question about the repetition, the teacher described how one year the children were particularly interested in their pets' feeding routines and pet nutrition; another year, the children were particularly interested in diseases pets could get, and they set up a veterinary office in the classroom to care for sick pets. The third year the teacher did the project on pets, the children were especially interested in the buying and selling of pets and set up a pet store in the classroom. And the fourth year, the children became interested in the breeds and breeding of different kinds of pets. In each of these cases, it was the interest of the children and the availability of experts among the parent community that enabled the pet project to take such different directions in terms of the main interest that developed.

Time of Year

When the teacher first becomes acquainted with a new class of children, it is helpful to choose a topic that most of the children have experienced personally and are ready to share with others. For example, families, babies, or homes are topics that are very much a part of their everyday lives. The openness that can be fostered at the beginning of the academic year is well worth developing early because it facilitates the teacher's understanding of individual children. Understanding is important for building relationships that help the children feel secure and through which they can be helped to explore their classroom environment with confidence.

VISITS TO PLACES OF INTEREST

Some advance planning is desirable if it is appropriate to arrange a field trip to a place of interest, such as to a local store or to a farm or even a walk around the school neighborhood. It is usually a good idea for the teacher to visit a site on her own before taking the children to it. Information obtained by phone or letter rarely provides enough detail to serve as a basis for preparing the children for a productive class visit. When the teacher makes an initial visit, she is likely to see points of interest in all kinds of unanticipated places. Consider, for example, visiting a park to gain firsthand appreciation of the opportunities it offers to people living in the neighborhood. In addition to what the teacher already knows about the park, a preliminary visit may yield useful information related to the interests of her own class. For instance, one group of children will appreciate the patterns in the wrought-iron gate at the entrance to the park; another group might prefer to read the signs on the trees and walls; and one or two individuals may want to spend most of the time studying the birds on the pond.

The staff of a department store, railway station, or clinic may find it difficult to visualize in advance the invasion of 20 young children. The teacher can help allay their anxiety and promote their understanding of what she hopes the children will gain from the experience. When a visitor comes to talk to the children in school, it may also be important for the teacher to explain in advance what she expects the children to gain and what they will be like to talk with. When given the opportunity to question a policeman who had finished speaking, one young child felt compelled to tell the man about his aunt's parrot that had just died, not quite appreciating the role of the police in relation to such small-scale disasters.

Elementary students appreciate the value of basic academic skills when they are able to see how these are important to adults in almost any workplace. The study of a business, whether a car wash, a sign maker, a restaurant owner, a local TV station, or a trucking company, reveals that they all involve working with words, writing, numbers, measurement, design, customer service, personnel, buying and selling materials, and so on.

The children also benefit from learning about the sense of responsibility that visiting experts convey as they talk about their work. For example, one expert who trained dogs to be suitable service dogs for disabled people brought his own trained dog to an elementary school classroom. From a wheel chair, he demonstrated the dog's ability to help its owner in various important ways: to open the refrigerator door to fetch the owner a drink or to pick up a pen off the floor when the owner dropped it. He also told how the dog was a demonstration dog as well as being his family's pet dog. There was a clear distinction for the dog about when it was being asked to work and when it was being "just a family pet dog." The work of training service dogs involved more understanding of canine psychology and health, as well as the needs of handicapped people, than at first might have seemed the case.

CHILDREN MAKING CHOICES

Choice can be a very important general feature of project work. Many teachers find that where opportunities for children to make genuine choices are increased, children's interest and commitment increase correspondingly. Project work offers children the opportunity to make choices at several levels, each with different educational implications. Some choices are procedural, some aesthetic, and some functionally intrinsic to the activity. Choices have implications for learning in cognitive, aesthetic, social, emotional, and moral areas. Varying in importance, some choices may have no far-reaching effects, but others may result in the success or failure of a major effort. Some options may be freely available, while others may involve negotiating with the teacher and/or other students.

Whatever the nature of the choice, the children can consult the teacher for advice, thus giving her an opportunity to talk with them about the work and to share her views and expectations. The practicalities of offering choices to children during project work can be thought of in terms of several options: choices concerning what to do and when, where, and with whom to do it. Whether to do something and for what reasons are very often matters that the children negotiate with the teacher. Each of these questions is discussed below.

Choice of Work to Do

There are clear limits on the extent to which a child may choose whether or not to undertake a given activity. A child cannot, for example, be allowed not to learn to read or write. However, many other more specific activities might be offered as genuine alternatives; similar tasks can often take very different forms. Writing a letter, a story, or a factual description of an event may equally develop the skill of writing. A sequence of drawings with captions may be presented in an accordion book, in a book with conventional pages, or in a pie chart presentation of a cycle, such as "Things I do every day." Books may be of different dimensions, shapes, or types and may include different content.

The teacher can be alert to the range of activities that children undertake to ensure they do not miss out on many enriching experiences. Children who regularly refuse to paint or to make models might need help overcoming their resistance; we have reason to believe that young children benefit from acquiring a broad range of expressive skills. Refusals may present an occasion for the teacher to ask the child why he or she does not want to participate. In this way, children learn to become accountable for justifying and explaining their choices. Through project work, the teacher may be able to suggest alternative learning activities that can be undertaken in different ways for different purposes.

Choice of When to Work

Children also have the opportunity to choose when to carry out tasks. So long as a particular piece of work is undertaken within a given period, two days for example, a child may choose to do it sooner or later, at the beginning of the time period or toward the end. Each choice has advantages and disadvantages, which can be discussed with the children. Discussion may lead them to favor completing one task early and another one later. Sometimes a child may be among the first to attempt a piece of work; at another time, the same child may prefer to wait and see what other children make of the same task before attempting it themselves.

In one case where the teacher offered the children a fairly open assignment, some of them sought the challenge of having the first try, while others waited to build on the earlier attempts. From watching their classmates, those who waited learned alternative ways of approaching the activity. Because there were several different responses to the task, learning was much more than mere copying. Children who did copy, however, discussed which model to copy. The following detailed description of this example illustrates the kind of learning potential offered by many open-ended tasks.

The activity consisted of painting checkered flags on large pieces of white paper for props in a play. The first child produced an interesting abstract design of randomly placed rectangular black shapes of different sizes. Immediately after having seen the first child's design, a second child painted rows of black rectangles separated by white spaces. Two days later, a third child painted alternate black and white squares row by row, producing the conventional checkered pattern. This child, a slow-moving and deliberate person, spoke to the teacher conspiratorially as she came to see him painting: "I have been thinking how I would do this," she said. But because the squares were quite small, she experienced difficulty sustaining the alternate squares pattern so that it lost coherence lower down the page as the squares became farther apart. Finally, a fourth child built on the third child's idea but made his squares bigger so that he had fewer to complete before filling the page and successfully maintaining the pattern. It was notable that no child spontaneously tried painting vertical and horizontal lines and subsequently filling in alternate squares or boxes, as an adult might have approached the task. During the three days over which this work was undertaken by different children, a considerable amount of mathematical language was used to describe and compare the products. Had the teacher instructed the children to use the more efficient adult method, the opportunity for the mathematical discussion would have been lost. Clearly, there was no single right way of carrying out the task.

On another occasion, a map-drawing activity (a map that included small drawings of items located at different places) that a few children had undertaken was discussed at the end of the day. Early the next morning, three of the children whose work had been discussed asked whether they might try it again. Their second attempts showed a marked progression in complexity and cohesion. Had they been required to wait until some later time before being allowed a second try, some of the interesting developments in their work might have been lost. Within the balance of activities, however, it was important to make sure over a week's time that these children did not spend a disproportionate amount of their time drawing or, if they did, that the same thing would not occur repeatedly.

Choice of Where to Work

Within one classroom, different kinds of space can be created in which children work: lighter or darker; more open or more confined; facing other children, the wall, or a window; working with a group of others or on one's own; standing, sitting up at a table, or lounging comfortably on cushions on the floor. Sometimes a direct relationship exists between the task and the chosen place, such as painting at an easel. On other occasions, the relationship is not so direct; a piece of writing might be undertaken in an open area or in a small space, with or without other children close by.

Children can learn that alternative settings have different benefits to their work or to their mood at the time. Some children's choice of where to work is best curtailed for a period of time by the teacher. When the beneficial effects of working in different places are discussed with children, they can understand the reason for the teacher's advice or demand. General recognition of such alternatives helps children make thoughtful choices that support their efforts and facilitate their learning.

Choice of Co-workers

At this early age, friendships are constantly forming, developing, or breaking down under the pressures of classroom life. Important discoveries are being made about what is involved in friendship, communication, cooperation, collaboration, and conflict. Young children vary greatly in the range and quality of interpersonal experiences that they have had outside of school. Social difficulties that persist throughout the early years of schooling are likely to cause pain and to reduce the quality of life for a person during that time and perhaps for several decades beyond it.

Children can be greatly helped by teachers who offer alternative strategies for solving social problems. Through project work, children can develop social competence through opportunities to talk, work, and play together in the classroom. Cooperation and collaboration can be encouraged by presenting appropriate problems to children. Some children prefer to work privately on making a book of their own. For others, the work is undertaken with much more enthusiasm if it is prepared by a group to be presented as part of a display. The teacher can encourage children to work under both conditions, helping them to see the benefits to be derived from alternative working arrangements. The following account gives examples of activities requiring negotiation and collaboration.

After visiting a large local garden center (nursery), a class of six- and seven-year-old children was given a two-meter square of white cardboard (packing material pasted together with kitchen paper). The square was spread out on an area of the floor cleared for the purpose. The activity was preceded by a brief discussion of what the children had seen at the center and what items might be included in a large collaborative painting. Only three procedural instructions were given: (1) three children were to work together for a short period (unspecified), (2) each child was to paint one or two items in the total picture, and (3) each child was to give up his or her turn to another child who had not yet made a contribution. The children took their turns, shorter or longer ones, and painted their ideas in the available spaces, which became smaller as the work progressed.

At least two-thirds of the class participated in the activity. The final result showed the care taken to preserve the unity of the picture. The items, of which there were many, were roughly in proportion to each other and observed the general rules of spatial relations, such as above, below, at the side, and in front. Items included the closed-circuit TV monitor, the check-out counter, a set of patio furniture on display, and shelves of watering cans, gardening gloves, ornamental dried flowers, feather dusters, bug sprays, packets of seeds, sacks of compost, potted plants and cut flowers, and many figures representing customers and workers. The overall effect was movingly suggestive of the place the children had visited as a class on the previous day.

The teacher intervened only toward the end, not without some trepidation, to suggest that the children see what the picture would look like if they filled the gaps between the objects with a "wash" of some sort. They tried using a pale yellow ocher. The overall effect was pleasing, and the whole class was happy with the result. It must be said that this work was achieved later in the school year, after the children had developed social skills that facilitated collaboration in the classroom.

The project approach offers children a learning environment that can develop their sense of their own competence and worth. It creates a classroom ethos in which children's points of view are taken seriously and their feelings and opinions treated respectfully. It offers the opportunity for children to try out their developing powers of judgment and to learn with confidence from their mistakes. The children's use of judgment can be practiced in situations calling for negotiation and decision making where genuine choices can be made. "Choice" is itself a neutral term, however. If the alternatives to choose from are of little educational value, then motivation is unlikely to be enhanced. The available alternatives must be carefully thought out and monitored by the teacher.

SUMMARY

The temporal structure of a project as it develops over three phases was outlined in this chapter. The principal features of the project approach were described with practical examples. These features have a role to play in each of the phases and were also discussed in terms of their value for the teacher in guiding the project work. In many cases, we have described events in the classrooms of teachers experienced with project work. Our description of the teacher's role discussed planning criteria of the development of a project and outlined the value of different kinds of choices that can enliven and personalize the work for children.

Throughout the period of initial planning, teachers find it useful to identify the key events that might occur in the life of the project, for example, a visit, a speaker, displays, central activities to be undertaken by individuals or groups, products of the work undertaken, and a culminating event to draw the work to a close. These events are described in some detail in chapters 4, 5, and 6. Once the preliminary planning has been undertaken, teachers can implement the project during the phase we call "Phase I: Getting Projects Started."

THREE

Issues in Selecting Topics for Projects

To a large extent, the benefits of project work are related to the topics on which the projects are focused. However, the number of possible topics is so large that the use of some kind of selection processes is advisable. Teachers have the ultimate responsibility for topic selection in that they must judge whether those selected are appropriate to the children's intellectual development and whether they are worthy of children's time and energy. Furthermore, to support good project work, teachers must often undertake extensive preparation, study, and exploration. Therefore, it is a good idea to determine whether the topics are of sufficient substance to warrant both children's and the teacher's efforts. This chapter addresses the issues involved in the selection of project topics and offers a list of criteria that teachers have found useful for topic selection in a wide range of settings.

ISSUES IN TOPIC SELECTION

Many factors are worthy of consideration when determining the appropriateness of a topic. For example, much depends on characteristics of the particular group of children who will carry out the work. Another factor might be the teacher's own knowledge and experience related to the topic, as well as her own interest in it. Still another consideration is the specific context of the school and its larger cultural community and physical surroundings. The availability of local resources related to the topic is yet another potential selection factor to consider.

Other criteria of appropriateness of project topics include their potential interest to the children, their possible contribution to children's sense of competence in dealing with and understanding their own daily experiences, and their possible contribution to later learning. However, it is a good idea to keep in mind that predicting which topics will work well is not simple, and many experienced teachers have been surprised both by those topics about which they had doubts that turned out to be beneficial, and vice versa.

In this chapter, we discuss some of the more complex issues that topic selection raises and conclude with a brief list of recommended criteria.

Children's Interests

Extensive experience of working with teachers implementing the project approach around the world indicates that their first consideration in topic selection usually concerns their children's actual or potential interests. Issues raised by this strategy are taken up below.

Following Children's Interests

Teachers sometimes select project topics on the basis of the children's expressed interest in them. However, while this strategy can yield appropriate and enriching topics, basing projects on the interest of an individual, a group of children, or a whole class can present several potential pitfalls in topic selection.

The first issue this strategy raises is: What does it mean to say that a child or group of children, or even a whole class, is 'interested' in a topic? The term "interest" in this context is not entirely clear. Interests can be of relatively low value (e.g., how to pull the legs off the fly [Wilson, 1971]); or they might be passing thoughts, fleeting concerns, phobias, fetishes, obsessions, or topics nominated by a child who is motivated by a desire to please the teacher.

Second, just because an individual or group of children expresses interest in a given topic (e.g., dinosaurs or pirates) does not mean that the topic deserves to be supported and strengthened. It may happen that children become interested in pirates after having seen an entertaining movie about them. In such cases, the children can be given opportunity for spontaneous dramatic play involving pirates, they can be encouraged to discuss their reactions to the film, and so forth. But such interest does not imply that an in-depth *investigation* of the topic of pirates is in their best developmental, educational, or even moral interests. We suggest that there is an important distinction between providing opportunity for child-initiated spontaneous discussion and play around a topic and a teacher investing a great deal of energy in organizing a long-range study focused on it, and thereby according the topic greater value than it warrants.

Third, we suggest that the topic of a project be part of the general commitment of educators to taking children and their intellectual powers seriously and treating them matter-of-factly and straightforwardly as young investigators of worthwhile serious phenomena. Our experience of working with many teachers on projects suggests that there is a general tendency to underestimate children's capacities to find the persistent hard work involved in close observation and data gathering of everyday phenomena around them satisfying and meaningful.

Fourth, adults have the responsibility to educate children's interests. Children's awareness of the teacher's real and deep interest in a topic (e.g., the changes in the natural environment over a six-week period) is likely to engender some level of interest in that same topic among the children who look up to her and respect her.

Finally, in a class of more than 20 children, the number of possible "interests" is too large to address in any single year! How should it be determined which of them should be addressed in the project work? Again, the teacher carries central responsibility for selecting the project topics and making all the related decisions.

Exciting Children's Interests

Sometimes adults promote exotic and exciting topics for projects in the hope of capturing the attention of children, especially those who often seem reluctant to join in the work of the class. For example, projects revolving around the rain forest undertaken in schools located on the U.S. Northern plains may very well entice young children into enthusiastic participation. We have also observed many projects in several countries focused on medieval castles where there are none, typically achieving animated participation by young children—at least for a short period of time. Similarly, we know of several teachers who have responded to young children's lively spontaneous discussions of the sinking of the Titanic, stimulated by a movie and television documentaries. While their interest was certainly palpable, the topic does not lend itself to first-hand investigations. However, good discussion and reading, led by the teacher who helps them interpret the new knowledge, would be appropriate in such cases, especially as the children grow older. Furthermore, though such topics do no harm, our experience indicates that young children can be no less absorbed and intrigued by the experience of close observation and study of their own natural environments, whether they are living prairies, corn fields, apple orchards, or a nearby bicycle shop.

Children do not have to be excited, fascinated, spellbound, enchanted, or bewitched by a topic. One of the potentially valuable contributions of good project work is that it can strengthen children's dispositions to be interested, absorbed, and involved in in-depth observation, investigation, and representation of worthwhile phenomena in their own environments. It may be helpful here to keep in mind the distinctions between *excitement* and *interest*. Excitement is a condition in which basic processes like heart rate, breathing rate, and pulse rate are increased for a brief period of time. Interest, on the other hand, is a condition in which each of these processes slow down except information processing and concentration of the experiences and stimuli at hand. Good project work depends on extended deep interest in a topic and its subtopics and persistent pursuit of answers to their own questions rather than on brief or momentary excitement.

Furthermore, if the topic of a project is an exotic and therefore remote one, it is difficult for the children to contribute to the direction and design of the work to be undertaken. In principle, the less firsthand experience the children can have in relation to the topic, the more dependent they are on the teacher and other adults for the

ideas, information, questions, hypotheses, and so forth that constitute the essence of good project work. Young children are indeed
dependent on adults for many important aspects of their lives.
However, we suggest that project work is that part of the curriculum in which children are encouraged to take initiative in setting
the questions to be answered, influencing the direction of the work
to be undertaken, and in accepting responsibility for what is
accomplished.

Along similar lines, topics are sometimes chosen because they are
expected to amuse or even entertain the children. Such topics are
thought by teachers to stimulate children's imaginations (e.g., topics
like *The Little Mermaid*, teddy bears, or the circus). However, these
topics are more fanciful than imaginative, and they are unlikely to
provide contexts for direct investigation and observation. In good
project work, children have ample opportunity to use and strengthen
their imaginations. This happens when they make predictions before
taking a field trip about what they will find when they get there,
when they predict the answers to the questions they will put to experts on the topic they are investigating, and when they argue with
each other about possible causes and effects related to the phenomena under investigation. Project work stimulates and strengthens
young children's imaginations also during the early phases of a project, when they are encouraged to report their own memories and
actual experiences related to the topic and to retell their own stories
related to them (e.g., stories of actual experiences of riding a tricycle
or going traveling on a bus).

Diversity Concerns

Diversity of Experiences

In some classes, the diversity of the incoming pupils' experiences
might be so great that it would be beneficial to *begin* the year with
a topic that the teacher is reasonably certain is familiar to all the
children in the class. A sense of community in the class is more
likely to develop when all the children have sufficient experience
related to the topic to be able to participate in discussion with some
confidence, to be able to recognize and relate their own relevant

experiences. For example, all children will have repeated experiences of food, though possibly a variety of kinds and preparation. Thus, a teacher could suggest to the children, depending on their ages, that they could collect a variety of kinds of information related to food in their own homes and neighborhoods and share their findings with their classmates.

As the school year progresses and children become adept and accustomed to project work, they can more readily appreciate the fact that individuals and groups have different interests and prefer to work on different topics or subtopics. In this way, they can learn to share with the whole class what each of them has learned. The diversity of work can stimulate and deepen children's appreciation and prizing of differences in experience, interests, and abilities among their peers.

Diversity of Culture

As defined and recommended throughout this book, the project approach is a highly appropriate way to respond to the diversity of cultures within the group of participating children. However, we find it useful to make a distinction between a child's *culture* and a child's *heritage*. The former, a child's culture, refers to the current day-to-day experiences and environment of the children; the latter, their heritage, refers to historic and ancestral attributes associated with their origins. In the early years, projects are most likely to be enriching if the topics are taken from the children's *culture* rather than *heritage*, though aspects of the latter can and should be introduced to the children in other parts of the curriculum. Not all of the topics of importance to children can be taken up in the form of projects.

Relationship to Curriculum Requirements

Most official curriculum guides are cast in such broad terms that it is usually possible to select good project topics from among the lists of knowledge and concepts mandated or recommended in local or state required standards. Making the relationship between the topic of the project and the prescribed curriculum requirements explicit for the parents can help reassure them that their children's education conforms to official guidelines. For example, in one fourth grade project on the rivers in the state, the teacher listed the competency benchmarks for environmental science, physics, science as inquiry, social studies, local geography, economics, etc., so that the children and the parents were aware of the official academic value of the work accomplished in the project.

Preparation for Participation in a Democratic Society

One important consideration we propose in the selection of project topics is a commitment to helping children to ultimately become competent participants in a democratic society. In the interest of this goal, good topics would be those that deepen children's understanding, knowledge, and appreciation of the contribution of others to the well-being of their larger community.

Secondly, in the interests of the goal of preparing for ultimate participation in a democracy, we ask: Will the study/topic strengthen and/or deepen a taste or disposition for close examination of real phenomena and their complexities? Can we overcome apparent reluctance to examine the real complexities about which we must make decisions?

Third, one of the many benefits of project work is that within the classroom itself, contexts are provided in which many processes and skills useful for participation in a democracy occur. Good project work provides contexts for developing agreements on actions to be taken, sharing responsibility for carrying out plans, resolving conflicts about findings, making suggestions to one another, prizing the different ways individuals can contribute to the total work accomplished, and so forth. In the more formal parts of the curriculum, children rarely have such early experience of these democratic processes.

Relationship of the Topic to Subsequent Learning

In many cases, the knowledge gained by children working on a project would be learned or "picked up" later on in other ways. For example, all children eventually learn the fundamentals about the behavior of shadows, or the basics of what goes on behind the scenes of a supermarket. Thus, one could ask why these might be worthwhile topics for young children.[1] We are not claiming that the process (e.g., of studying the behavior of shadows) is more important than the new knowledge the school curriculum introduces or requires. We suggest that educators at every level are responsible equally for both the value of the processes and the content involved in children's work. Although in the case of project work, we are not primarily concerned with a particular product or pre-specified knowledge-acquisition outcome, all of the kinds of learning we are concerned about—skills, dispositions, and feelings—should be addressed while investigating worthwhile topics. While project work provides pretexts, texts, and contexts for a wide range of important skills and dispositions to be strengthened, ideally these experiences occur in the course of investigating worthwhile topics.

Delicacy of the Topic

Some topics are potentially delicate because of their religious or cultural implications or because they might in some way offend some of the families served by the preschool or the school. Some topics might also be delicate in the sense that they touch on matters individual children may not want to share their experience of. For example, some children might not want to talk about their own houses or even their own families. The teacher can evaluate the potential delicacy of a topic as she comes to know the children well.

Clinical Considerations

Occasionally, a teacher is responsible for an individual child or small group of children whose personal situations are such that a topic ordinarily appropriate would not be selected in order to address the special case. For example, many teachers of young children have guided them through detailed study of the local hospital. However, it might be the case on occasion that a child has had a very recent traumatic experience—perhaps losing a loved one—or a frightening hospitalization experience of her own, suggesting that the study of that topic might best be postponed until a later time.

Pressures for Accountability

Can the knowledge and skills gained contribute to addressing demands for accountability and meeting local or state standards?

Sometimes teachers attribute restrictions concerning topics for projects to district curriculum requirements even though, often, no such restrictions are actually there. Occasionally, teachers indicate that they are conducting particular lessons because the state or district requires them to do so, even though such requirements do not actually exist. It is thus a good idea to check carefully in advance concerning recommended and mandated subjects and topics.

A Tentative List of Criteria

Based on the issues raised above, we offer a tentative set of criteria for topic selection as follows:

A topic is appropriate if:

1) it is directly observable in the children's own environments (real world);

2) it is within children's experiences (most of them? some of them?);

3) first-hand direct investigation is feasible (and not potentially dangerous);

4) local resources (field sites and experts) are favorable and readily accessible;

5) it has good potential representation in a variety of media (role play, construction, graphic, multidimensional, graphic organizers, etc.);

6) parental participation and contributions are likely; parents can become involved;

7) it is local-culture sensitive as well as culturally appropriate in general;

8) it is potentially interesting to many of the children or an interest that adults consider worthy of developing in children;

9) it is related to curriculum goals of the school, district, etc.;

10) it provides ample opportunity to apply basic skills (depending on the age of the children);

11) it is optimally specific—not too narrow and not too broad (e.g., a study of the teacher's own dog or "buttons" at one end, and the topic of "music" or "the seasons" at the other). However, the narrow topics could occasionally provoke good mini-projects.

SUMMARY

The selection of project topics is ideally negotiated in discussions of the teacher with the children, even though the teacher has the ultimate responsibility for it. Furthermore, no matter how interesting a topic might be initially, it could happen that over time, interest in it might subside. Depending on the ages of the children involved, the teacher could talk to them at group time about whether they are ready to bring their study of the topic they have been working on for some time to a close. If there is apparent strong interest in continuing the investigation, then the teacher can support it. If there appears to be general agreement that they are ready to bring the investigation to a close, the teacher can encourage them to suggest what closing activities they would like and how and when to prepare for a final Phase III concluding event.

It is ultimately up to the teacher to monitor the children's involvement and to determine when it might be advisable to bring the investigation to a close or whether it might be necessary to introduce a fresh aspect of the topic to re-stimulate interest.

Investigating a Variety of Aspects of Food

All children can be encouraged to deepen their knowledge and understanding of food and related phenomena by means of a good extended project investigation.

A project related to food should go well beyond the usual listing of "favorites" and cutting out pictures of various foods from newspaper advertisements. The listing of favorites of almost anything can very soon become boring. It also tends to turn children's attention inward to themselves rather than to their larger environment and diverse as well as shared experiences!

Phase I. Getting Started

The suggestions about a possible project related to food are based on experiences with three- and four-year-olds. While in these examples, the teacher raised the initial question concerning children's dislikes of foods, she usually wrote down their responses and main points on a flip chart or black/white board, and thus the children seemed to take the questions seriously and to become deeply involved in the project topic.

Early interest in the topic of food was provoked with a question like: What are some foods you don't like? Chances are most preschoolers respond with considerable interest to that question and fairly easily become involved in seeking answers to it. This can be followed with:

• What don't you like about them?

Here the teacher can introduce terms such as:

• Is it the taste, the smell, the color, the texture (i.e., is it too slimy, crunchy, creamy, etc.?)
• Is it bitter, sweet, spicy, salty, etc.? Each of these terms can be studied empirically in the preschool environment.

Some other questions the teacher can use might be:

• What are the likes and dislikes of others in your household?

Depending on the ages of the children, they can be encouraged to nominate possible answers and to create a survey, making a preliminary list of possible likes and dislikes that can be followed by a box in which to mark a "Yes" or "No."

The children can be encouraged to fill out the survey forms at home with family members, interview nearby neighbors, family friends, and others with whom they have informal contact, or even to raise the questions during a phone call.

Some other kinds of questions the children might seek answers to in such a project:

- Which food items have to be cooked before being eaten?
- Which items can be eaten raw?
- Which foods can be eaten both raw and cooked? (Possible Venn diagram)
- Which food items have to be peeled?
- Which are usually chopped? Grated? Mashed? Ground?
- Which have to be stirred? Baked? Boiled? Broiled? Grilled? Fried? Poached? Barbequed? Steamed? Or all of the above?
- Have you ever noticed:

  - What gets soft when it is cooked? (e.g., potatoes, apples) and which foods get hard when cooked? (e.g., eggs, dough)
  - Which foods change color when cooked? (e.g., butter, meat)

- What things do you swallow that are not food? (e.g., Pepsi, cough medicine)
- Conduct surveys at home to answer questions like:

  - What foods are stored in the refrigerator?
  - In the freezer section?
  - In a cupboard? Cabinet? Etc.?

- Which foods items are stored in cans?

  - In cartons?
  - In boxes?
  - In jars?
  - In bottles? Etc., etc.

- What are some differences between

  - a jar and a bottle?
  - a box and a carton?
  - a vegetable and a fruit? Etc.?

- How many kinds of cereal are there at home?

  - How many can you count in the supermarket?

At sometime early during Phase I, let the children's parents and main caretakers know about the topic to be studied and solicit their help with the surveys.

Phase II. Collecting the Data

The teacher can help the children (depending on their ages) to develop surveys they can take home. Some children will be able to complete the simple surveys themselves. Others will need the help of adults at home. In addition, they can develop plans to put their questions to those related to their school or their program and those who take responsibility for their refreshments and/or meals.

Phase II can include visits to a local grocery store, a bakery, etc., and/or a supermarket. It can also include inviting a chef to show them how various foods are prepared, etc.

Make sure most of the children have mastered the vocabulary suggested in the list above, or as much of it as possible. Some of the children will know more of the terms and their meanings than others. But all of them can learn from each other in arguments and discussions together. Encourage them to take satisfaction in their new knowledge of what goes on around them related to something as fundamental as food.

Phase III. Bringing the Project to a Close

As the survey data and drawings are collected, the children can be engaged in discussions about how to share the story of their investigations. The documentation and display of charts, Venn diagrams, drawings, and photographs taken throughout the investigation should reveal their findings. Children from other classes as well as their families can be invited either to a formal presentation of the story of their investigation or to simply enjoy viewing the documentation of the story of their work.

NOTE

1. Note that the opposite is also true: much that is learned through formal instruction in school that is thought to be essential to later life or to "cultural literacy" is forgotten soon after the instructional episodes.

FOUR

Phase I: Getting Projects Started

The organization of projects into three sequential phases helps teachers and children to identify the main tasks as they unfold and to deepen the sense of direction and purposefulness of the work. As indicated in previous chapters, Phase 1 includes introducing and clarifying the topic and subtopics to be investigated, sharing experiences and knowledge related to it, and specifying the list of questions the investigation will attempt to answer.

Some projects claim the children's interest from the first minutes; others require more effort from the teacher. Not all children will be equally interested in all topics. However, the way the teacher introduces the topic of the project can be an important factor in determining how the project progresses and what is achieved. In this chapter, we discuss various ways of engaging children's interest and participation when launching a project in Phase 1. We begin by considering ways of involving children during the preliminary discussions in the earliest stages of the project. Next we describe types of activities that are particularly appropriate for getting projects started. These are followed by suggestions for involving parents. We conclude the chapter with a section distinguishing Phase 1 for the elementary school years.

ENGAGING CHILDREN'S INTEREST

Children's attention and interest are easily aroused by the new and the unexpected. This is especially true when they can relate the new to something they already know. A brick, some mortar, a detached faucet, or a doorknob can raise interest immediately, because they look strange when detached from the houses children live in. Similarly, objects that children may have seen only at a distance, for instance, a wheelbarrow, a bicycle, or a sewing machine, can offer much to observe and talk about. Entirely new objects, such as an oar from a rowboat, a beehive, or a blood pressure gauge can also be intriguing. The culture of the classroom where projects are undertaken encourages children to be curious about new things or familiar objects in new contexts.

Pictures can often provide a good stimulus for discussion and interest, especially if they are related to the objects presented. For instance, items of house construction might be accompanied by pictures of builders, plumbers, or electricians at work. Similarly, the medical equipment might be shown in a picture-story sequence of a sick child going to the hospital for treatment and getting well again. A brief slide presentation can also be a good introductory stimulus, especially if there are plenty of opportunities to follow up on children's questions afterward.

When the project being introduced follows other previous projects, the children can be reminded of relevant events and experiences that had been particularly enjoyable. They might look forward to similar occasions in connection with the new project. The sense of a common group history strengthens the sense of community, and the teacher can do much to encourage this in simple, incidental ways. For example, a study of the neighborhood may include a walk around the streets close to the school. The teacher might remind the children how interesting they had found their walk to the supermarket earlier in the year during the project on buying food.

Introductory Discussion

The initial discussion of a project should make a strong impression on the children. It is a good idea to present them with a provocation that is engaging, arousing their curiosity and inviting interest. The teacher might tell a story from personal experience related to the topic, and one or more related objects might be displayed or passed around the class. Open discussion about the topic reveals the degree of familiarity the children already have with the topic. Their views and comments about particular items are welcomed.

In the early class discussions, teachers will find it useful to let children recount events in their own experience related to the topic. For instance, in a hospital project, many of the children will be able to talk about their own accidents that resulted in a visit to the hospital. Helm, Beneke, & Steinheimer (2007) describe the beginning of an elaborate, in-depth study of the mail system undertaken by a group of 3- and 4-year-olds arising from listening to a story entitled *A Letter to Amy* (Keats, 1968), which tells of a boy named Peter sending a letter to a girl named Amy. After having listened to the story several times, the teacher engaged the children in discussion about how the letter might get from Peter to Amy. The discussion revealed to the teacher the extent of the children's knowledge, experience, understandings, and misunderstandings of the mail system and provoked their interest in learning more about it and developing one for their own school. The project involved all the children in the class over a period of six weeks (see Part III in Helm, Beneke, & Steinheimer (2007) for a full description of the project).

The initial discussions of most topics usually generate what is called *script knowledge*—namely, knowledge about sequences of events leading to a goal—which many children use spontaneously in their dramatic play. Children can also be encouraged to talk about their play and their use of the equipment. As they articulate their need for some new props, such as a bag for the mailperson to carry letters in or a stethoscope or bandages in an investigation of the hospital, the teacher can encourage them to design and make what they need or to acquire real items.

At the beginning of a project, the children's enthusiasm is usually easily aroused. It is therefore important that enthusiasm be kept at an optimum level to avoid setting expectations so high that they might not be met. Undertaking a project is a serious matter, and steady involvement on the children's part is required to achieve much of the work planned. Indeed, as we have suggested in Chapter 1, project work provides contexts for strengthening important intellectual dispositions, such as to become involved in sustained effort, to seek information, to make predictions, to test hypotheses, and to share findings.

In the initial discussion, the children should be invited to think about the project and aspects of the topic they want to explore and learn more about. The teacher and children can think of items they might collect from home to display on walls and horizontal surfaces. Over the following few days, the children can be encouraged to volunteer or sign up for which parts of the work they would like to undertake.

During the early discussions, the teacher finds out the language and knowledge at the children's disposal for talking about relevant experiences. She learns how the children can already talk about the topic and where they might have difficulty expressing their ideas and questions. Sometimes clear misunderstandings and conflicting impressions are exposed, leading to animated exchanges among the children. The teacher should not be too ready to correct children in the group situation, since this may inhibit participation in the discussion. Instead, the teacher's approach at this point might be to draw their attention to the opportunities they will have to find out more and to clarify their understandings.

Throughout the first week or more of a project, the children can reflect on their experiences related to the topic and share what they have experienced with the other members of the class. This sharing requires the children to first reflect on and represent their experiences in some way. Depending on their ages, they can tell stories, write, make graphs and charts, draw pictures, label drawings, make paintings or collages, make clay models, construct with blocks, role play, and so on.

Older children can also investigate each other's experience through interviewing each other and conducting surveys to find out about each other's experiences. Depending on their ages and previous experience, this research of their classmates involves children in rehearsing interview techniques, taking notes, data collection, and representation of the group's experience in graphs and charts of various kinds.

The teacher's role is to support the use of a variety of investigative and representational strategies. She also has a special responsibility to probe the children to reflect on their experiences and explain them. As children explain their experiences, they develop theories about how and why things are the way they remember them. Up to this point in a project, a great deal of interest can be aroused in the topic because the children are the experts. They know what they have experienced, and they can reflect on what they know. For example, in a discussion of their experience of the supermarket, children might wonder about where the money goes that is paid at the checkout counter. Some might think the clerk takes it home as her pay, others might think it goes to the manager, others might suggest that it gets taken to the bank at the end of each day, and still others might think it is used to buy more items for people to buy in the store. One question arising from such a discussion might be, "What happens to the money the people give to the store clerk when they buy their groceries?"

Throughout this process, they wonder about the different experiences and explanations their classmates offer. The teacher's ethnographer role extends to coordinating the work produced so that the children can all become aware of what has been learned and can appreciate a collective baseline understanding, which can be the foundation of the collaborative research process ahead of them in the second phase of the project. During the initial discussions, the teacher can suggest activities, some of them to be undertaken by individuals and others by small groups working together. Suitable activities are discussed below.

ACTIVITIES FOR THE FIRST PHASE OF EXTENDED PROJECTS

When a project is planned to last for several weeks, there is time to allow for qualitative change in the activities as the work develops. In the beginning, however, relatively unstructured activities are most helpful to the teacher in assessing the children's prior understanding. Dramatic play, painting, drawing, and writing from memory about personal experiences related to the topic are suggested activities. Each of these is discussed in turn below.

Dramatic Play

If the classroom does not have a play area, it would be a good idea to start one. A square of inexpensive carpet or matting can be laid in a corner of the room to designate a small area. A three-sided screen with a door in one side and a window in another can also be placed there. Because it is flexible, this basic arrangement can become a farmhouse, a hospital, a hot-air-balloon basket, a camper, or a boat. The teacher and children can discuss how to prepare the play area for a suitable topic related to dramatic play. The children are likely to be very interested in the transformation of the area from one project to the next. It is a good idea to encourage the children during these discussions to make suggestions to each other; not all the children's questions, comments, and suggestions have to be directed to the teacher. Discussions involved in project work are ideal contexts in which to encourage the habit of child-child interaction; during group meetings, children learn to listen to each other's ideas and suggestions rather than just sit and wait until it is their turn to talk to the teacher, ignoring other children's contributions.

For the present discussion, the theater term "props" is used to refer to objects that the teacher introduces to enrich dramatic play. Dramatic play is particularly enhanced if the children have real objects as props. The children's understanding of events is reflected in the way they use the objects that are part of those events. Props also enable the children to replay the sequence of events that takes place in the real world, for example, to role-play the scripts related to hospital events, shopping in a store, or buying stamps in a post office. It is best to provide a few familiar props during the first phase of a project so that the children can easily explore their own associations with the topic. As project work progresses, less familiar and completely novel objects can be introduced and added into the context of the project.

To illustrate the points made above, let us look at the hospital project. The play area can become a hospital with a row of dolls in cribs, a child-sized cot, a chair, a dresser, and a sink. Props can include plastic medicine bottles, an arm sling, and bandages. It is a good idea to add steadily to the props throughout the life of the project. Later additions may include X-ray pictures displayed against a window, a thermometer, patient charts, a stopwatch, a bed pan, a wash basin, nurse and doctor uniforms, and various doctor's instruments. The quality of the play changes across the three phases of the project, and the functions fulfilled by the props become increasingly useful in refining and elaborating children's understanding.

From observations of children at play, the teacher can identify understandings and misunderstandings. The following examples of misunderstandings have been reported: "The doctor makes you better when he puts the thermometer in your mouth" and "I'm going to be a doctor when I grow up, because then I'll never get ill." Such revelations can provide information that can be used to clarify understandings in later group discussion.

Children have to accept certain conventions or precautionary rules about not putting things in their mouths, not using large instruments near their faces, having no more than six children playing in the hospital at one time, and the like. Such rules are usually readily accepted when the reasons for the precautions are clearly given. Some rules can be generated by the children themselves to solve practical problems that emerge during their play.

Drawing, Painting, and Writing

Because various kinds of art media and writing are important ways of representing and communicating understandings, teachers can encourage children to apply these skills in project work. The effectiveness of communication can best be judged in relation to the people to whom the message is addressed. Project work can offer opportunities for children to communicate with their coworkers in small groups, with the class group, the teacher, parents, and with children in other classes.

Bulletin boards can be used to document different aspects of the project so that the children can see the story of their own work. The teacher can ask the children to suggest where and how their experience and their work should be displayed. She can also use many opportunities to draw children's attention to items on display. She can ensure that some aspects of the display change frequently so that the children continue to notice what is there (see Helm, Beneke, & Steinheimer, 2007).

Children can work individually or collaboratively in preparing documentation and reports of their work. For example, a group might construct a "wall story," which is an illustrated sequence of events depicted in paintings and writing. The story might be about a child who has an accident and goes to the hospital for treatment. This is another representation of a script. It can be displayed near the play area so that the children can refer to it in their role play. For example, a dispute about the order of events arose among some children playing in the class hospital. Together they consulted the events depicted in the wall story to settle the dispute. In that case, the disposition to resolve disagreements by checking "the facts" can be expressed and satisfied.

Children will be able to draw and paint pictures of the events they remember from their own experience of illness or accident. In one class, the teacher found that all of the children had a story of some sort to tell about how they had hurt themselves. She suggested that they write and draw their stories and collect them in a book called "Accident Stories." In this way, children can read about the real things that have happened to them.

ENCOURAGING THE PARTICIPATION OF PARENTS

Parents can be involved in project work in at least four ways. First, because the topics of projects are likely to be familiar to the parents, they can easily discuss their own experience and knowledge with the children. For instance, children can ask their parents whether they have been to the hospital. A kindergarten class studying bicycles collected stories from their parents about bicycle accidents they recalled from their early experiences. In a project about "Water in Our Houses," kindergartners asked parents to show where the water is heated in their homes. Some teachers particularly welcome the opportunity to speak to parents as a group about their intentions for children's project work during the year. In this way, they can prepare the parents for the children's requests for information and other contributions to the project.

Second, parents can be encouraged to ask their children how the project is progressing, what activities they are undertaking, and about their findings so far. Often, parents find it difficult to obtain intelligible replies to questions about what their children are doing in school, especially in some areas of the curriculum. In project work, however, the teacher can help the children talk about their work at home by suggesting events and aspects of the work to discuss with their parents. In so doing, the teacher establishes communication and accountability with parents. Communication gives the children an additional opportunity to practice the new language they are learning in school. Parents also learn about aspects of the curriculum associated with the application of skills and the development of dispositions that are likely to help the child work well in school. Certain skills and dispositions in particular are generally less well understood and appreciated, for example, the dispositions to persist in the face of difficulty and to vary the problem-solving strategies when first attempts fail. Documentation of such experiences can help further the parents' and community's appreciation for the role of dispositions in a wide variety of achievements.

Third, the parents can be very helpful in providing information, pictures, books, and objects to help the whole class in its pursuit of knowledge on the topic. Sometimes a parent who is a doctor or a nurse is willing to talk to the children during a health-related project. A father who is a mail carrier may come and talk about his work and bring some items from the post office. Parents can assist in arranging a visit to a factory, a farm, or a store. As part of project work, the children can write letters to take home with questions asking for specific information, such as common childhood diseases they have had and at what ages. For a project on babies, the children may find out when they cut their first teeth or learned to walk unaided.

Fourth, at a later stage of the project, parents might be invited to come and see the children's work. Each child can guide his or her parents around the display areas, and the class can sing a song or put on a small play they have written. Such visits help parents gain confidence in the school and in their own contribution to the child's continuing informal education at home. Parents can thus feel involved in an important part their children's school life.

THE CLOSE OF PHASE I

The first phase usually ends with a clear and agreed-upon set of questions and a shared sense of what kinds of investigations are planned that will help to find answers to them. Many teachers learning to implement the project approach with young children have reported having difficulty getting the children to nominate research questions to be answered in Phase II. Indeed, for many young children, their most common school experience is of being asked questions rather than posing them—though throughout the second and third years of their lives, questioning adults and others is one of their most common characteristics!

Teachers can help children regain their dispositions to pose questions by engaging them in discussions on the project topic by asking the children to talk about such things as:

a) What they want to find out;

b) what they want to look at more closely;

c) what they want the visiting expert to talk about, tell them, or show them;

d) what they want to know more about; and

e) what parts of an object they want to draw in detail or want to take photographs of.

Discussions around these topics encourage children to discuss their questions and predictions. During such discussions, the teacher can then say something like, "I see, so one question you want to ask is. . ." and thus rephrase the child's expressed interest in what she or he wants the visitor to talk about.

One of the best ways to get questions asked is to explore current experience. Take the example of a project on the topic of the seashore. As teacher and children explore the things they have personally experienced, such as ocean beaches or creatures you can find on the beach or in rock pools, the teacher will find the children have gaps in their knowledge and some incomplete or erroneous ideas about crabs, shells, or fish. As these become apparent in the discussion, it is possible for the teachers to question the children with a view to helping them clarify their thinking on a topic.

It may be very important during an early discussion not to tell the children whether their answers are right or wrong or to give them information. First comes a time of speculation and theory exploration. It is a time for the teacher to take an ethnographic role, with a genuine interest in finding out what is in the children's minds and helping them to construct a common or agreed basic understanding. This may be a very inadequate one. If you live in a landlocked state or province, the children will have even wilder or more primitive ideas about crabs. The topic in this case may not be such a useful choice. If you live near the ocean, however, inevitably some children will know more than others.

Early discussion of the topic can become lively if the teacher, as the lead thinker, models how to think about and review past experience. The teacher might say how she found her first hermit crab and what she observed. Then there is usually a child who will want to join in and tell about his/her experience, then another child, and so on. The aim at first can be just to get the children keen to talk about the topic from their own experience or even from their own speculation.

The teacher can also model "wondering." For example, she might say, "When I think of that hermit crab I first saw, I wonder if it was trying to get back into the water. I wonder how long they stay out on the sand. Perhaps I should ask someone who knows. I should ask somebody that question." Then the teacher would make up one with the children. It may sound as though it could be a little laborious when described like this, but it really is not so. Often it happens that all the children want to chip in and contribute to the discussion.

Then, as the discussion becomes more animated and richer in detail, the teacher can help the children formulate some questions about what they might need to know more about and who might be able to help them find out more. Discussion of the questions can also include the participating children's predictions of what the answers to their questions might be. The teacher can help the children develop a table listing their questions and their predictions. This record can be referred back to later once the children have found out answers from field site visits or expert visitors to the classroom (examples of question tables are to be seen in Chapters 8 and 9).

SUMMARY

Observation of children at play and at work can inform the teacher of understandings and misunderstandings. She can also learn about the children's preoccupations or concerns, such as their mothers going into hospital to have babies. Sometimes children play out anxieties that can be shared and alleviated. Children may also develop interests in some part of the topic through their play. An interest in the heart or bones can be followed up by reference to books, observations of a lamb's heart, pictures, X-rays, and so forth.

Toward the end of the first phase and the beginning of the second, the teacher can look back at her web plan of the project and evaluate different parts of it in light of what she has learned about the children so far. By the end of the first phase, a field trip will have been arranged, or maybe an invitation has been issued to a visitor who can respond to questions they will plan to put to him or her. The teacher then begins to prepare the children for this event by talking with them about the kinds of things they can expect to see and learn.

FIVE

Phase II: Projects in Progress

The main thrust of the second phase of a project is research, which is seeking answers to the questions formulated at the end of Phase 1. In this way, Phase II consists of a variety of ways of gathering data and gaining new information. In this chapter, we discuss preparations for field work and the types of activity typically included in Phase II to help obtain and organize the data gathered by the children. A selection of activities that children can undertake in pursuit of a fuller understanding of the topic is discussed together with opportunities to practice skills and encourage desirable dispositions. The products of children's work are discussed and how they can be used to reflect learning and stimulate further questions. We also suggest ways the teacher might support the children's continued interest in the project, extend the challenges for more able children, and structure special opportunities for children with learning or motivational difficulties.

PREPARATIONS FOR FIELD WORK

When the children have agreed on the main research questions at the end of Phase I, a discussion about possible places to visit and visitors to invite begins the second phase. At this point, children can volunteer to work in small groups on specific subtopics. The teacher may then organize focal events, such as a field visit or a number of appropriate visiting experts. These events can provide important sources of questions, information, and ideas of interest to the children. Group discussions are a valuable way to prepare children for a new experience and to debrief them afterward by helping them to share their understandings of new information.

Group Discussions

Discussions with the whole class and with smaller groups working on specified subtopics have both informative and motivational functions. At the beginning of the project, discussions enable the children to share what they as individuals know about the topic, and they enable the teacher to explore the children's present understandings. In the second phase, discussions have several additional functions: to prepare the children for field work, classroom visitors, or other key events; to help children refine their questions for investigations; and to plan the next steps and other future work. In discussions, the teacher helps the children share the thoughts and experiences they are having, thus promoting the community ethos in which the work will thrive as she sets expectations and guides activities.

Young children's discussions are most likely to be fruitful when they have interesting and mind-engaging content. When they feel involved with the content, there is less need to repeat the rules of hand raising, turn taking, and attending. Children will listen to others because they want to hear what is being said. The teacher's talk can consist of comments as well as questions (chapter 2), and children can be encouraged to interact with each other so that not all of the conversation directly involves the teacher. One way to manage such discussion among children is for the teacher to ask them to make suggestions for a group's plan or answer classmates questions. So, for example, in a class doing a project on a construction site, the group in the class that has elected to collect data on the types of building materials used can be asked by children in other groups studying other subtopics (for example, kinds of workers, types of rooms being built, and so on) to be sure to include questions they also want answered. As the work in the second phase progresses and discussions of the progress being made are held, the teacher can take opportunities to encourage children to pose questions to each other and to encourage, and even to congratulate, each other on what is being accomplished. If the teacher asks questions in turn of each group or of each child, and the children only answer her directly and are not encouraged to exchange questions and suggestions with each other, it is likely that they will tune out of the whole process as soon as their "turn" to talk is over.

The teacher can also take notes at these discussions and turn children's attention to their own earlier ideas and comments by rereading to them what they had said and asking them about their further thinking on the subject. In this way, the teacher can provide a model of an interested listener for the children. Her comments on the children's talk also model appropriate replies and reflections on what another person says in a conversation.

Some teachers report that they find it difficult to get young children to pose questions. It may be that asking the younger children if they have any questions leaves them a bit confused about what is expected. However, if the teacher asks the children, for example, before an expert is due to visit their class, "What would you like the veterinarian to talk about?" or "What would you like the bicycle mechanic to tell you about or to show you?" then the children are more likely to suggest ideas than can be reworded as research questions.

Sources of Information

In projects for preschool children, the main field work is obtaining information by means of firsthand direct observation and experience. It also includes looking things up, gaining ideas, and copying words and diagrams from relevant books. With increasing age and greater skillfulness in using various media, the sources of information can be expanded to include secondary sources as well as primary ones. Primary sources include field work in real settings, observations of events and activities, work at an actual construction site to be observed, the operations of various machines related to the topic, or the goods delivery section of a supermarket.

Interviewing people who have direct experience of aspects of the topic also provides information about other people's firsthand experiences. Secondary sources of information, such as books, magazines, newspapers, relevant educational films, videos, brochures and pamphlets, and websites accessed via the Internet can be examined at this time as well.

FIELD VISITS

During Phase II, a field visit can be planned by the children and teacher together. Field visits do not have to be elaborate, involving expensive transportation to distant places. They can involve going to places close to the school, such as stores, parks, construction sites, businesses, or community services. With the use of teacher's aides, the children can go to these sites in small groups, enjoying the opportunity of having an adult to talk with about what they are observing.

Young children collectively can be interested in almost every imaginable aspect of a trip outside the school. Few details escape their notice if the teacher, together with the children, has made clear the expectations for the main purpose of the trip. The teacher can encourage awareness of the more routine aspects of the visit, such as arrangements for transport, meals, and groupings of children with particular adults. These routine aspects give the children practice in classifying, counting, and representing pictorially and symbolically the events of the day.

For example, older children can write descriptively in the following manner: "There were twenty-seven children and five adults on our bus. This was thirty-two people from our school and thirty-three people altogether with the driver. The bus had forty seats for passengers, so eight seats were empty." Inevitably the children will be interested in the mode of transport and the food, and these interests can provide useful opportunities for teaching and learning. Of course, the teacher can also draw the children's attention to features of the visit that are pertinent to the main work of the project. The younger children can dictate their impressions for the teacher to record.

The preparatory work completed before conducting field work includes identifying questions to be answered, people to talk to about their work, equipment, objects, and materials that can be observed closely. Children can carry clipboards (small, lightweight, simple ones for the younger children) and sketch or write things of special interest to be used on return to the classroom. During the visit, the children can also be encouraged to count, note the shapes and colors of things, learn any special words for things, figure out how things work, and use all their senses to deepen their knowledge of the phenomena studied. Usually it is preferable to leave such on-the-spot recording open-ended. When the teacher supplies a checklist of items to look for or a list of questions to answer, children can be distracted by the "treasure hunt" quality in these activities. Instead, if she suggests only a few things to look for, the children can observe them closely and with interest rather than compete with each other to discover items on a common list.

Younger children's attention can be drawn to people or objects, their functions, how they work, and how they relate to other objects or people. The grouping of objects on the basis of common characteristics and their differentiation from other kinds of objects requires children to observe closely. Analytical discussion is encouraged, and later on in the classroom, the teacher can help the children represent their observations in various ways in pictures, charts, and writing.

Consider, for instance, a visit to a clinic. The children are likely to see a thermometer, blood pressure gauge, and stethoscope, all of which are instruments for diagnosing what is wrong with a sick person. The children are also likely to see surgical scissors, a hypodermic syringe, and forceps, which are used to treat a person once the problem is diagnosed. After the visit, a discussion can lead to the distinction between the two sets of instruments. The children's understandings of the two sets and how they overlap can be represented pictorially in a Venn diagram of two overlapping sets. The inclusive class of objects is labeled "instruments," and the distinction between the subsets is based on the difference between the functions of diagnosis and treatment. A small flashlight might be used for both. Children's labeled drawings can be grouped appropriately in the diagram, which can be displayed with a child's written commentary about the information summarized in the diagram. Other children might write questions that can be answered by referring to the diagram: "Which instrument is used for both diagnosis and treatment?"

"Which is the smallest instrument used for treatment?" or "Which instruments made of glass are used in diagnosis?"

If a museum is being visited, the children may be able to separate into groups, each with a particular interest to follow. Each group of maybe four or five children should be supervised by an adult who need not be a teacher. Parent volunteers can be briefed by the teacher to encourage observation and recording and to talk with the children about what they are seeing. Back at school, each group can report what they saw and noted. When children share with others who did not see the same things, there is a clear purpose to their communication, and the other children can be encouraged to ask questions to clarify their understanding.

Using illustrated books, the children can elaborate on their own sketches and fill out descriptions. More questions can be asked and answers sought. Often, new information leads children to ask more questions in school after the visit. If the museum is a local one, some children who visit it regularly with their families might be willing to make a weekend trip there to gather additional information needed. Otherwise, the children can write to the museum after a visit to clarify points that may arise back in the classroom.

Interest is strengthened when the topic is treated in the kind of depth made possible by direct experience of real-world settings. For instance, the mathematical skills of comparing, sorting, classifying, and ordering, which are often acquired and practiced in artificial and disembedded settings, can be applied to project work when the children study an item of real interest to them. Studying the parts of an ambulance, for instance, might lead to a comparison of the materials in it: metal, plastic, wood, and fabric. The substances that make the engine work—gasoline, oil, water, and air—can be compared in various ways according to their function.

If the teacher cannot take the children outside the school to visit an appropriate site, an expert may be invited to visit and bring objects or pictures to leave on loan to the class. Sometimes, when it is impossible to go outside the school for direct firsthand experience, something can be arranged within the school building or on school grounds. The school itself could provide a field study opportunity in the context of a project on food, buildings, people at work, etc. A walk around the school can afford much information for discussion. The teacher can ask the school janitor to accompany the children on a tour of the school, showing them where the materials and equipment used to clean and maintain the building are kept. If school meals are cooked on the premises, the children can see what is involved and observe the people who do the work.

ACTIVITIES FOR LEARNING

Upon return to the classroom from a field visit, the children can recall many details and represent them in increasingly elaborate ways as they learn more about the topic. At this time, the children apply skills already learned—talking, drawing, dramatic play, writing, mathematical notation, measurement, diagrams, etc. If the field site is close by, such as a construction site in the vicinity of the school, it can be visited on several occasions, and comparisons can be made between what was observed on one visit and on subsequent ones.

As the project progresses, children can undertake a wide variety of activities, which are discussed here under three headings: construction, investigation, and dramatic play. We also discuss various ways that children can apply the basic academic skills of language (talking, reading, and writing), mathematics, and science to each of these types of activity.

Construction Activities

As children build models, they ask questions about design and construction. The models can be made of junk material, clay, and wood, as well as from construction toys, kits, or other materials. Children can talk about what to include in their model; for example, they can discuss the parts of the ambulance, both outside and inside. They can talk about the problems they are solving as they construct the model—how to fasten the wheels on, the scale of the model, and how to fit all of the necessary items inside. Finally, they can discuss the finishing touches, such as the red cross and the lights to complete the model to their satisfaction.

Basic skills, language arts, and mathematics are applied in activities related to the construction. These activities are enriched when the children can read about the ambulance, for instance, in books and study detailed pictures of it and its functioning. The writing of older children about the object they are constructing may be of two kinds. First, they can report how they made the model and describe the materials, strategies, and techniques that failed and succeeded. This writing might be collected in a class book about model construction or displayed alongside the model itself. Second, the children can write about events involving their ambulance: a journey to pick up a sick person in an emergency, an accident, or the life and work of an ambulance driver. This writing might form part of a display showing different aspects of the work of the hospital.

In mathematics, many activities related to the construction of the ambulance can be undertaken. Parts have to be measured to fit together, and relationships of width, length, and height can be considered. Some mathematical understanding can add depth to the construction of the dashboard with its dials and gauges.

Investigation Activities

The primary purpose of investigation activities is to find out information. After being introduced to the topic, children who have gained confidence in what they already know about it can be encouraged to go further, to find out new information, to build on their basic understandings. New places and objects can be explored, and questions can be asked. The teacher can help extend the children's repertoire of active investigation strategies. In the classroom, children can hypothesize, estimate, and experiment. For example, in a study of the manufacture of clothing, children can find out about different fabrics by designing a test to compare fabrics for insulation or waterproofing efficiency. They can try to simulate some of the processes involved in producing fabric for clothing by growing, collecting, and cleaning cotton, wool, or linen. They can try spinning, dyeing, or weaving yarn or thread to make cloth.

Receptive strategies that children can use to investigate a topic include observing, listening to an expert, watching someone at work, and reading. Observation involves looking closely at objects, handling them, and maybe using other senses. Instruments used by doctors, tools used by builders or plumbers, and equipment used by cooks can all be studied closely, and the cause-and-effect relations implicit in their use can be noted, for example, the shape of the parts of a stethoscope for picking up and transmitting sounds, a syringe for injecting, and a hospital bed with mattress, pillows, head-rest, and progress chart for accommodating a patient.

Observations can be set up over a period of time so that changes can be noted, measured, and recorded. Growing plants in the classroom offers such opportunities, as do studies of the weather, animals, and birds outside the classroom window. Recording observations in drawings, writing, and tallies enables children to reflect on the learning involved in the observation. This can be further represented in mappings, charts, and graphs.

Investigation can often be motivated by construction activities. The older the children, the greater their concern with realism in their constructions; for example, the relative height, width, and length of the ambulance being built may become significant.

Dramatic Play

Dramatic play can be stimulated after a field trip by adding new props such as X-ray photographs and patients' progress charts. New scripts can be learned, such as visiting a sick friend in hospital; going there to have a baby, an operation, or a broken bone set after an accident; and the roles of doctors and nurses in these scenarios. New understandings of the functions of objects and people are reflected, and new misunderstandings noticed and clarified.

Dramatic play in the second phase involves trying out new information in context. Children rehearse the new understandings embedded in situations that they can be helped to imagine through accounts and stories, thus making their own best sense of the topic. Role-playing activities can lead directly to questions. Children may want to know the journeys typically made by the ambulance in the area or in a given period of time. According to the age and understanding of the children, such investigation provides opportunities for work on direction, time, speed, and distance. In studying the work of the ambulance driver, the children might chart or map the places the driver goes in one day to pick people up or take them home or to another hospital. The ambulance driver may also have considerable training in first aid to offer emergency help, such as giving oxygen or carefully positioning a person with a broken limb on the stretcher.

Products of Work

The work that the children produce might include pictures, pieces of writing, charts, graphs, models, and board games. These products can be stored in personal folders or mounted in individual books. They can be displayed in a class book focusing on one aspect of the project. They can be displayed on vertical and horizontal surfaces such as walls, windows, tables, and shelves. Children's work displayed under subthemes or particular aspects of the project serves various functions for the teacher and the individual child, as well as for the whole class.

The wide range of task complexity usually accompanying project work offers very able children an excellent opportunity to undertake challenging tasks suitable to their ability. Likewise, it offers an interesting selection of important but much simpler tasks to children who have learning difficulties. Teachers can help structure the tasks and advise individuals about how to apply their skills to maximum effect. This strategy is likely to strengthen children's motivation to collaborate with other children as they are able without fear of being shown less competent. The following example illustrates this point.

A small group of children were working together on a picture of an ambulance. They wanted to display it with strings running from different parts of the vehicle to word labels around the outside of the picture. Two children wrote the labels, one measured and cut suitable lengths of string, and the third pinned the strings in place. The child who pinned the strings would have had great difficulty writing the labels, but his contribution was valued because he performed a necessary task. At the same time, he improved his reading ability while matching the words and objects.

CLASSROOM DISPLAYS

Display areas devoted to the project can be major focal points for classroom-based activity as the work develops. During the first phase of the project, displays give children the opportunity to collect, sort, represent, and share current understandings of a limited range of relevant items. As the project progresses, the emphasis shifts to three other functions of display: (1) to provide information that children can refer to in their work and play, (2) to document children's growing experience of the project and show a developing record or diary of the work, and (3) to communicate the children's discoveries and achievements to particular audiences (their own teacher and classmates, other teachers and classes, the principal or head teacher, parents, or any other visitors to the school).

During the second phase of the project, these functions of display become still more important. Each function is discussed below.

Displays for Information

Displays are most informative when they include key words for children to use in their writing. In this way, they serve as a specialized glossary or vocabulary list. The children can compile an alphabetical list for reference in addition to the easy-to-see labels of objects on display (all letters should be lowercase for young children). Pictures, photographs, reference books, maps, charts, and a small selection of commercially produced material can be displayed for information. Children's own pictures and writing can also be informative, as well as imaginative or reflective. Various pictorial and symbolic representations are undertaken specifically to present discoveries in an organized form that enables easy retrieval of facts by other children needing the information.

Bar graphs can present frequency information. Venn diagrams provide a mapping of information in sets of objects that have some similarity or are parts of wholes. The same set of objects that are parts of a thing can be classified into subsets according to different attributes. For instance, an ambulance has parts made of metal, rubber, glass, wood, plastic, and fabric. These same parts can be classified differently according to whether they are part of the transport function of the ambulance or the health emergency function. As the children gain experience in analyzing items in project work, they are more likely to suggest ways of their own for presenting information to others. When tasks differ from child to child, achievements should be shared so that the new understandings can benefit other members of the group. An informative display is particularly interesting when it depicts things that the onlookers have not personally experienced but that they can easily assimilate in terms of what they already know.

Displays as Documentation

The second function of displays during the second and third phases of the project is to provide documentation recording the life of the work as it develops. The contributions of individual children and cooperating groups provide a growing source of information about the achievement of the class. The teacher uses this documentation to reflect back to the children the progress they are making in their investigations. Children can be fully involved in discussion and planning what will be displayed and how. They become familiar with the displays and take pride in their own and each other's work. In doing so, they are motivated to assimilate the new information where it enriches what they already know. They are also motivated to rework and accommodate their understanding to information that conflicts with their earlier concepts.

The shared and public meaning of things is given due status by display. The documentation of the children's work around the classroom is formally useful throughout the life of the project as a record of the achievement of the class for the teacher, the principal or head teacher, the parents, and other interested parties.

Displays to Communicate to Outsiders

The third function of displays is to offer children a place to communicate what they would like to tell others about their work. This function overlaps with the documentation function. It is, however, different in a very fundamental way. When displays are used as documentation, some of the charts and observations children make are part of their investigation of an object or event. In contrast, when displays are intended for communication to others, children sometimes write a description of their own work and say what it adds to their personal understanding of the topic. They can write for children in another class, for older or younger children. They may develop a quiz or a series of questions that can be answered by referring to a graph or to a mapping of groups of items.

To return to the ambulance example, a quiz for older children might include this question: "What is the largest thing that is made of rubber and is part of the health emergency function of the ambulance?" And for younger children: "What is the smallest metal instrument used by the doctor in finding out what is wrong with the patient?"

One of the best ways a person can be sure of understanding something is to try explaining it to someone else. When explaining things, we have to put ourselves in the mind of the other person and predict what we will need to say or write to ensure understanding. Children can write captions for graphs and diagrams that explain to other children how to extract information, or they can write or dictate to the teacher instructions for games. Children can design and make simple board games for two players on some aspect of a project.

For the hospital project, they might design a dice and track game where some of the squares or positions on the track represent getting sick or having an accident, while other squares represent possible remedies or help from medical personnel. Setbacks for patients can be indicated by the instruction to "miss a turn" and positive gains by the instruction to "take another turn." On a different topic, one group of children explained their playground games in writing so that others who had never played these games could learn by following the rules. Another group tried them out and offered ideas for improving the instructions.

The children's work can be accumulated in individual project folders, on wall displays, and in group record books in which work is shared with others. The information collected from interviews can be represented in various similar ways. The work can also be stimulated and enriched by a variety of secondary source materials, books, charts, leaflets, maps, brochures, and pictures.

THE TEACHER'S ROLE

The scene is set for the project during the first phase, when the teacher evaluates the children's levels of understanding and interest in the project. In the second phase, the class revises and enriches their understandings on the basis of firsthand experience through visiting an appropriate location, looking closely at objects, discussing real events, and talking with people who are involved with the setting being studied. The teacher orchestrates the learning events, shaping the overall outcome of the project. Some of the activities the children can be engaged in are painstaking and slow-moving, others spontaneous and short-lived. Some play is open and free, other activity highly structured and focused.

In this second phase, the teacher is strengthening the children's dispositions to be resourceful, independent, imaginative, involved, cooperative, and productive. The timing of when to provide resources is related to activities the children can undertake, optimizing interest where possible. Timing is important in maintaining the momentum and depth of the work. The following is an example of judicious timing in a study of two tortoises.

During the project's first phase, lasting one week, the children observed and recorded the physical parts and attributes, activity, food intake, and behavior of one female tortoise. In the second phase, lasting two weeks, a male tortoise was introduced. The children then made a comparison study of the two animals, reviewing their understandings of the female and comparing in detail the female with the male. Thus, the study had two purposes: (1) finding out about one tortoise and (2) comparing two tortoises. Had the teacher introduced the two tortoises at the same time, the amount of interest would have been halved, since activities that were repeated with a new purpose would have been undertaken only once with both purposes lumped together.

We do not wish to suggest that the activities described in this chapter usually happen spontaneously in work on projects. They do not. However, the teacher can use many ways to help children engage and persist in construction, investigation, and dramatic play. Children can be encouraged to ask questions and think about the possibility of alternative answers. They can be helped to see how observation can lead to questions, which in turn can lead to experiments. They can be taught how records of observations can be translated into reports of discovered information. Children can gain personal satisfaction from increasing their competence. They can appreciate the products of their efforts, as these contribute to a record of learning for the whole class. The teacher is instrumental in promoting the classroom ethos, which enables children to cooperate, appreciate one another, and share the work of their class with others.

Compared with work produced through systematic instruction, the standards, complexity, length, level of difficulty, and precision in project work tend to vary considerably among the children's achievements, because the children do not always work to the limits of their ability. Some will be free-wheeling, while others will be working at a level far beyond their customary performance, owing to some special interest in the activity. The teacher can be instrumental in ensuring that the more mature and more able children are sufficiently challenged by their work. She can also find many opportunities to motivate less able children in the varied classroom context that the project approach affords. Standards may vary among the different pieces of work produced by any one individual in the same project. The teacher notes these differences and monitors the general performance of individual children over time.

Although the teacher continues to have an active role in the second phase of the project, the orchestration of learning consists in her being responsive to children as they attempt to solve problems and to master tasks. They need encouragement when their confidence weakens, suggestions when they run out of ideas, answers to their questions, direction to other sources of information, or new objects to boost their interest. The enthusiasm that accompanies the initial stages of the project should be replaced by a sustained interest and satisfaction in the work being accomplished.

SUMMARY

In this chapter, we have described the development phase of a project. The main emphasis here is on giving the children new experiences through which they will be able to pursue the questions they generated in the first phase of the project. Various ways to help the children prepare for a field visit were discussed, as well as strategies for helping children learn as much as they can from the firsthand experience that a field site offers. Following the field visit, there are many ways for children to continue their investigations in the classroom. Both primary and secondary sources of information are important in the second phase of a project as children work on various representations as they document what they have learned and help other children with their growing understanding of the topic. Specific reference was made to the value of representing new knowledge in construction and dramatic role play. Older children can represent what they have learned using diagrams, maps, timelines, Venn diagrams, and graphic organizers of various kinds. In the process of representing new knowledge, children continue to investigate further questions about the topic. It was noted that the classroom walls and bulletin boards can be very helpful in documenting the progress the children are making in their research. Completed samples of children's work on display can also offer models of different forms of representation that can be used to share new knowledge. It is important that teachers encourage the children to share and appreciate the good work being done and to be helpful to one another in setting and achieving appropriate and satisfying standards. As the children continue to investigate the topic and work on representations, class discussions can help them think about the topic in many interesting ways that stimulate purposeful activity and involve the use of various skills. In the second phase of project work, the children are learning to monitor and evaluate their own efforts and achievements. They can learn to ask each other for advice, to discuss strategies, and to consult as they work together.

As the work progresses in Phase II, the children often develop a strong concern for realism and logic about the topic, and drawing real objects becomes an increasingly absorbing activity. In their observational drawing, young children can look closely at how the parts of a bicycle interconnect within the whole, note how the pattern inside a carrot dissected different ways indicates the way water and other nutrients contribute to its growth, and so on. Interest is stimulated by frequent recognition and review of the progress being made in the development of the project. In the next chapter, we discuss the value of drawing in each of the phases of a project.

SIX

Phase III: Concluding Projects

Sooner or later, projects in the classroom have to be concluded, even though children can be encouraged to recognize that learning on any topic is never really finished; there is always more to learn. A topic is merely set aside until the next time it is encountered, either within or outside the school context. Various approaches to concluding a project are discussed in this chapter.

CONCLUDING PROJECTS WITH YOUNGER CHILDREN

For a class of preschoolers, the decision to end a project can be made by the teacher in consultation with the children. The teacher takes into account play around the project constructions and materials. If frequency and quality of play have declined to a low level, she may ask the children whether they are ready to dismantle the project or set it aside in some special way. Similarly, if the play ceases to change, develop, or be elaborated after a week or two, the teacher can discuss with the children their readiness to end the project. If no new props are added, or if constructions are not extended after a week or two, the children may have exploited the topic as much as they want to at that particular time.

The teacher may then suggest that the children contribute drawings, paintings, or stories for a class book about their work. If the project included a large construction, the children may be interested in organizing guided tours to explain their work and other aspects of the project to children in other classes. The children should discuss and agree in advance and in some detail what they will show, recount, and explain to the visiting children and parents. When the time comes to end the project, it is a good idea for the children to take responsibility for dismantling it themselves, preserving some elements and saving materials that can be used for subsequent projects.

Small groups of children can arrange collections of the photographs in narrative sequences to mount on background construction paper. They can dictate or write appropriate captions for themselves to go with the photo sequences. In this way, the children participate in documenting their experience. In the course of this process, the children can come to achieve greater depth of understanding and clarity about what has been learned. The Phase III documentation processes provide a type of review and summarizing that can help children's mastery of information and concepts associated with the topic. In one classroom, the older "buddy" class of fifth graders interviewed the children on their work. They wrote down what the children said about photographs and self-selected drawings taken from their project folder.

The class can also invite parents and others in the community to listen to presentations of the work of various groups on all the subtopics investigated and to view their documentation and constructions (see a description of the documentation processes used with 3- and 4-year-olds in Part III of Helm, Beneke, & Steinheimer, 2007).

CONCLUDING PROJECTS WITH KINDERGARTEN AND ELEMENTARY GRADE CHILDREN

Three aspects of the concluding phase of a project with children in kindergarten through third grade are discussed in this chapter. First, children can usually gain a sense of closure if the teacher and the whole class together develop a shared view of what they have learned and achieved during the project. This can be done by arranging one or more culminating activities, such as giving a presentation to other classes, to the whole school, or to parents and members of the community who are invited in to see the work at an open house culminating event or activity.

Second, it is a good idea for the teacher to monitor the level of the children's interest to ensure that boredom does not become widespread—an indication that the time has come to conclude the project. Ideally, interest in the project activities should be sustained, and everyone should remain at least somewhat involved in project activities until a collective culminating event has occurred. Many interesting strategies can be used to encourage children to elaborate and consolidate their newly acquired understandings related to the topic of the project. However, keep in mind that any topic, no matter how interesting it might be at the outset, can eventually be run into the ground.

Third, children should reflect on the work they have accomplished individually as well as in a group so as to appreciate their own growing competence and understandings. The teacher can help them evaluate the work accomplished and the evidence of their progress as the project evolved. Individuals can take stock of what they have learned about their own learning. They have new strategies and skills, as well as new confidence to bring to their study of the next topic. An awareness of their corporate learning can help children value the collaboration involved in so many of their activities. The teacher's role is crucial in setting the tone of thoughtful self-assessment during the final weeks or days of work on a project.

During the first and second phases of a project, much of the work should address the realities of the topic. The work should include observations, descriptions, experiments, and problem solving. The boundaries between the real and the imaginary, the probable and the fantastic can be clarified in the course of working on a project.

Once the children have acquired an in-depth understanding and relevant knowledge related to the main aspects of the topic, they are prepared to invent, create, and imagine characters and places for stories to write or dramas to perform. During the third and final phase of a project, activities that enable children to consolidate their understanding, applying newly acquired information in imaginary contexts, are appropriate. When these activities lose their appeal, the children are probably ready to move on to the next project.

CULMINATION OF A PROJECT

At all ages, the activities undertaken during the second phase of a project can generate interesting and informative products. As these accumulate in individual project folders, in class books, on shelves, and wall displays, they constitute a rich resource that serves as a communal documentation of the project's progress since its beginning. A different story can be told about each project. No two classes of children will ever develop quite the same ideas and interests, undertake the same tasks, or solve the same problems, even if they investigate the same topics. The uniqueness of each project reflects the distinctive thinking of each class of children and their teacher. A school assembly, an open house, or an invitation to parents and administrators to visit the classroom offers the teacher and children the opportunity to give an account or tell the story of the project to interested outsiders. The displays show achievements of the children, and each child can talk about his or her own work and the work of others.

Presentations to Other Classes

Where the whole school meets in daily assemblies, one day a week is often set aside for individual classes to talk to the other children and the teachers about their work. Sometimes a class can talk to just one other class about its work. Such communications enhance the children's feelings of belonging to a larger social unit within their school. The spirit of caring about the learning throughout the school community helps to create an ethos in which the older and the younger children respect and support each other inside and outside the classrooms. The older children first listen to the achievements and efforts of the younger children and then present what they have been working on in a way that the younger children can find interesting. In preparation for these presentations, the teacher can encourage the presenters to predict what elements of their experience and work are likely to be of greatest interest to others. They can also be encouraged to discuss and reflect on what might be the best ways to make their ideas, insights, and experiences clear to the intended audiences of older or younger schoolmates. The disposition to anticipate others' interests and to strive to make oneself clear to them is among the valuable dispositions to be manifested and strengthened during project work.

Some of the larger pieces of work, such as paintings, charts, and models, can be shown at these meetings. Selected children can describe how these items were made, the materials used, the difficulties encountered and overcome, as well as what they represent. Individuals might read a description, a story, or a poem they have written. A small group might put on a brief play while the rest of the class acts as chorus, singing or playing incidental music on percussion instruments. Or the whole class might sing or play music together.

The teacher can coordinate the presentation of these products of project work, narrating the story from both the children's point of view and her own. Preparing for a presentation is usually enjoyable and energizing for the children and offers opportunities to formally summarize the highlights of the project for individuals and groups. Class discussion takes on a reflective and summarizing function, helping the children to appreciate their own and others' achievements.

We want to stress that a presentation is primarily a communication rather than a performance. A presentation offers the children the opportunity to represent and share their experience with interested others, and it offers the other children, teachers, and parents the opportunity to hear about the experience. Entertainment is not the main purpose, although these occasions often have entertaining features. The event is intended to communicate learning, but it does not need to be a precisely learned, formally scripted, and formally rehearsed occasion. Opportunities can be provided for spontaneity and improvisation. If children are accustomed to this kind of experience from an early age, most of them will not be overawed by an audience. The emphasis here, as in other aspects of project work, is on engaging children's minds in the processes of sharing their learning. Children talk as much about the activity and about how they worked as they do about the products of their work.

These learning processes involve making models, writing stories, designing and conducting experiments, recording observations, representing information in graphs, and so forth. The emphasis is not primarily on the product, although the product is important as final evidence of the value of the process. Children can learn to explain, describe, report, and record the way they worked. For example, if two previous versions of a drawing were instrumental in achieving quality in a third and final version, the child can report how she or he modified each drawing in each successive effort. First drafts are not described as "mistakes" or as evidence of "where I went wrong" but, rather, in terms of "what I only saw at first," "when I realized," or "when I saw how I could do it differently" to achieve a desired effect. Children who describe their efforts in terms of trying out alternatives before attaining the most satisfying outcome are communicating the value of such an approach. They model an awareness of learning strategies for other children and show how their thoughtfulness contributed to the final work. Project work can thus strengthen dispositions to persist in the face of challenges and to strive toward learning and mastery.

Consolidation Activities

The process of consolidation involves applying the knowledge acquired in familiar situations to a range of other understandings. To illustrate the activities that facilitate this process, let us take a close look at a project on the weather. New knowledge is likely to have given children the sense that the weather is less arbitrary than they had previously believed. They may have come to understand better that many everyday happenings are directly related to the weather—clothing they wear, the washing being quickly taken off the clothes line, gardening tasks, roof repairs before winter, and the timing of a visit to the shops. Young children observe their parents doing many things for no apparent reason. Often adults do not make their reasons explicit even when questioned.

Consider this example: A sudden storm causes a father to rush out to close the windows of the car parked in the driveway. His four-year-old child, standing somewhat in the way, asks, "Daddy, why are you running?" The father might give one of several possible answers: "The car will get wet inside." "Mind, out of the way, I have to do this quickly!" "It's going to rain any minute!" "Look at those dark clouds over there!" "Your mother is upstairs!" "Get your tricycle in before the rain comes!" A one-sentence answer to a child's question about an event presupposes that the child has the background understanding necessary to make sense of the answer (even if it is not a non sequitur). The child might be left wondering, "Why will the car get wet inside?" or "It isn't raining now, how does he know the rain is coming?" and so on. In their dramatic play and through writing poems, stories, or captions for paintings, children can give reasonable explanations for familiar events in the light of their new knowledge about how the weather affects our lives.

Sometimes consolidation activities allow children to elaborate peripheral interests in the project. In the school bus project, for example, older children might draw a map of an imaginary town with its school and children's homes. They might set and solve problems about the "best" routes a bus might take, given the location of the school and the homes. Not all of the ideas will come from the teacher. The children might have many ideas themselves. The displays remain a source of information, and various tasks connected with them can still be undertaken. Where appropriate, information on display can be used in connection with tasks that test children's understanding. The displays at this stage might be refined for public view during an open house. Most of the work produced in the third phase can contribute to the children's own personal project folders, which form the records of individual progress.

Open House

Another form of a culminating activity is an open day or open house when the class can report on the project to parents, administrators, or other visitors. Children can give visitors a personal guided tour of the classroom, or they can make a more formal presentation along the lines described for the school meeting. It is a good idea to give parents the opportunity to see how their responses to the request of the teacher and their child have contributed to the project. If parents have been very involved, the visit will be especially interesting to them; if they have not been involved, it may suggest ways they can help in the future and may encourage them to do so the next time.

Evaluating the Project

At the conclusion of any project, it is useful for the children and the teacher to reflect on the skills, techniques, strategies, and processes of exploration that the children have used in the project work. All of these competencies can be applied with greater proficiency and confidence in a project on a new topic.

Much evaluation can occur when planning a culminating presentation, for instance, when the teacher and class discuss the various special events or group and individual achievements. If each of the children has been keeping work in a project book or folder and the teacher has been monitoring their progress, she will know which children require help to complete work and which would benefit from supplementary activities to clarify limited or erroneous understanding. Some teachers also find it helpful to encourage children to look back at their own work during the course of the project. For example, during Phase I, when the direction of the investigation is being developed, the children can make predictions about what their findings can be. During Phase III, they can revisit these predictions and speculate about the bases on which they made them, which predictions were close to the facts, which were not, and reasons for any errors.

Information on the bulletin boards can be used during this phase as a basis for formulating and responding to quiz questions. These can be a practical method of checking on the new knowledge that individual children have learned.

Children can also talk with each other and the teacher, either in a class group or individually, about the skills they have practiced in the project. The teacher can help to summarize these skills to ensure that they are more easily available when the children embark on the next project. For instance, if the children have counted frequencies for a survey, they may have tried alternative ways of recording items and counting them in groups or tallying them. They may have compared the efficiency of chunking the items in twos, threes, or fives. Discoveries about the most efficient way to count and record the results can be influential in similar situations in the next project. The skills can be practiced in subsequent surveys. The older the children, the more explicitly and deeply these kinds of evaluations can be discussed.

Teachers' records of individual progress throughout the project will vary in specificity according to the ages of the children. With the youngest children, few records may be kept. With school-age children, some schools require more extensive records than others. In school systems that require extensive or detailed records of children's progress, the teacher can list all of the activities undertaken by each individual, some of the groups, or the whole class.

For each child, a record can be developed that notes which activities were undertaken and the level of proficiency achieved. One approach is to compile a matrix with curriculum competencies on one axis and the main project work activities on the other. When a competency is used in a particular activity, a check mark can be entered in the appropriate cell in the matrix. In this way, the project activities can be mapped onto the competencies. As each child works on an activity, the appropriate check on the matrix can be circled. Thus, the competencies practiced can easily be seen. Keeping precise records of achievement is more complex with project work than with work sheets and standard tests. Nevertheless, teachers should not be discouraged from incorporating the project approach into their curriculum, as a much wider range of assessments can be made in the context of a project than in that of more traditional curriculum and teaching methods.

In addition, records of what the whole class accomplished in the project can be useful for future reference. The web that was devised in the initial planning stages can provide a framework for this record. Using different colored markers or some other method of marking, the teacher can note the activities accomplished, the visits made, the resources used, and the areas most fully investigated. She may also want to note aspects of the project that were least well developed. Activities or events that occurred but were not in the original plan can be added to the diagram.

An anecdotal account of how the web was expanded can serve as an additional evaluation of the project. A record of the whole project from the teacher's point of view is useful if she should wish to repeat a similar project and could be of interest to other teachers undertaking project work in a similar area. In some schools, records of this kind are kept on file as a planning resource. In this way, teachers can share ideas and make their experience available to each other.

WHAT HAPPENS NEXT?

As the work of a project draws to a close, the teacher sometimes recognizes a strong new interest emerging for the children. In the bus project, the children's dramatic play might have led to play about the bus taking them on a vacation. They might have considered what it would be like to go to different places, and they might have talked about where they had been and where they were likely to go later on. If this would be an appropriate project to do next, then the teacher might encourage the idea. The children might set up a travel agency, collect brochures, and make tickets to sell. The school bus construction, if not too dilapidated by this time, might be repainted as a tour bus, or be converted into a ferryboat, or an airplane.

Or consider the school bus project of the kindergarten children. Initially they might have focused on the bus itself, making models, experimenting with wheels and motion, and graphing the time required by different children to ride to school. They might have become interested in the various routes. This interest might then lead appropriately into a project on making maps of the neighborhood, thereby extending the children's graphic skills and increasing their knowledge of their larger environment.

Sometimes the teacher has an idea about which area of the curriculum she wants to emphasize in the next project. If so, she can begin sowing the seeds of new interests as she sees their potential for future project investigation developing out of the project now completed.

SUMMARY

The purposeful application of skills in project work opens up many possibilities for children. The classroom offers more interesting activities than any one child can ever do. Yet when a whole class of children takes advantage of these opportunities, all children benefit from the full range of activity available. In a project, individual children learn to be selective in pursuing their own intentions in an environment where learning opportunities abound. With the teacher's help, they learn to make responsible choices based on interest.

The third phase of a project is a time for elaborating new knowledge introduced in the second phase. It is a time to reflect on and evaluate what has been learned. It is also a time to look forward to new ideas and to the application of skills in the study of a new topic.

At the end of the school year, the teacher and children together can recall the more memorable events in the projects undertaken and reflect on the greater facility the children have acquired during that long period. In one school, the teacher and children made a class book at the end of the kindergarten year. The book included examples of individuals' work when they first started school. The children wrote about their early memories of school life and drew pictures of the events described. Each child could see how his or her own drawing and writing skills had advanced during the year. Through such activities, the children can become more fully aware of their increased competence and can be helped to look forward with confidence to the challenges in the year ahead.

SEVEN

Drawing in the Context of a Project

INTRODUCTION

Drawing can greatly enhance project work for children of all ages. Most work products, whether they involve writing, diagrams or other forms of representation, are more interesting and informative when accompanied by drawings. In addition, the processes of drawing are instructive in themselves. Drawing in project work is mainly draughtsmanship, or technical drawing, done to represent and convey factual information. However, there are also opportunities for the more artistically expressive kinds of drawing. Children can draw for a variety of different purposes throughout the three phases of the project investigation.

This chapter is presented in three main sections. In the first section, the contribution of drawing to children's learning is discussed. Second, several different kinds of drawing and their purposes are examined in relation to the development of projects. The third section describes teaching strategies for the teacher to encourage purposeful drawing in the context of a project. It will be readily seen that the contribution of drawing to children's learning is not limited to their use of it in project work but can enhance their work in many other aspects of the curriculum.

THE CONTRIBUTION OF DRAWING TO CHILDREN'S LEARNING

Drawing in project work can contribute to all of the four kinds of learning goals mentioned in Chapter 1: knowledge, skills, dispositions, and feelings.

Knowledge

Early in the life of the study, the processes of drawing help children recall the details of past experience relevant to the topic. Drawing enables children to retrieve relevant memories and gives them a focus for discussion with other children about the common and different experiences they have had. Once the children begin learning from firsthand experience and from secondary sources of information about a topic, drawing enhances the examination of detail. Drawing from observation requires children to look closely and make frequent checks with the real phenomena they are observing. In so doing, they discover detailed information about objects, events, people's roles, and the relationships of parts to wholes.

Skills

Drawing also provides children with an ideal language for representing complex ideas. In order to represent reality in the form of a drawing, some data reduction is necessary. Only the most salient details can be represented. This data reduction involves children in sifting through visual clues and selecting those that will best reduce the information to its essentials. This selection process can guide children's choices of words for oral or written language. Thus, drawing can help children with various aspects of linguistic as well as visual expression and communication.

Drawing involves a kind of problem solving, as the three dimensions of the reality of a car, a dog, or a mountain, for instance, are reduced to two dimensions on the flatness of the paper. Drawings can also be revisited, modified, elaborated, and labeled.

This process of revisiting is a reflective one, helping to make the experience memorable and deepen the learning. It also encourages children to try to draw an object on several occasions and work on improvements to their final product.

Dispositions

Drawing is a pleasant and intrinsically satisfying activity for most children. The desire to draw can energize children's work and provide opportunities to strengthen several dispositions of particular value to teachers. Five examples of such opportunities afforded by drawing are worthy of special mention here.

First, high-quality illustrations can contribute to the attractiveness and personal significance of project work. Children's experiences of ownership of their project work are enhanced by drawing because it enables individual expression in representational work. Second, since children value the results of skillful drawing, they will usually apply themselves willingly to practicing their drawing skills and techniques. Practice at drawing can be shown to produce small increments of improvement, which children can readily appreciate. Third, when children encounter problems in their drawing, they are often persistent and resourceful in solving them. Fourth, when children are in the process of drawing, their attention is most often especially focused. The resulting concentration often shows itself in children as a deep, calm absorption. Another explanation of this quiet absorption is that it is very difficult for anyone to draw and talk at the same time, perhaps because these activities make simultaneously competing demands on different functions of the brain (Edwards, 1979).

Fifth, the disposition to work hard at improving personal strengths is strong in those children who draw well, since project work offers many different opportunities for drawing to be useful and appreciated. Competence in drawing can be especially valuable to some children with difficulties in other parts of their achievement profiles. These children are helped in all areas when they can see their skillfulness in drawing contributing to the collaborative effort of a learning team or to the project as a whole.

Feelings

Drawing can build confidence and self-esteem, as it features children's strengths and encourages them to persist in following up their own ideas in the exploratory climate of the project. Drawing is another form of communication and one which opens new opportunities for children's ideas to be expressed and appreciated. There is also an aesthetic dimension to drawing, enabling the development of sensitivity to pattern and structure. In the classroom, many teachers have remarked on the power of drawing to help very active and impulsive children to focus their attention in a calming way.

THE CONTRIBUTIONS OF DRAWING TO THE DEVELOPMENT OF A PROJECT

Drawing can facilitate and elaborate the development of a project from its beginning to its conclusion. Children can apply drawing skills in projects to extend and enrich their work and give it a particularly personal quality. Whereas the systematic instruction of older elementary school children in art can help them to acquire new skills and extend their drawing activity, the application of drawing skills to project work makes very different demands on the children compared to the requirement to follow instructions in an art class. In an art class, the teacher may expect all the children to work on the same particular drawing skills at the same time. The enrichment of project work through a variety of different kinds of drawing at any time can be combined with other forms of representation to give them a particularly personal and individual quality. A discussion of different kinds of drawing tasks in each of the three phases of a project is presented to show how they can enrich the children's project work.

Phase I: Beginning a Project

In the first phase of a project when the children are discussing their own memories related to the topic under investigation, the representations they draw can provide the teacher with information about the children's personal experiences. The experiences they represent may be as recent as last week's shopping trip or as distant as an airplane journey two years earlier. Drawing from memory often lacks specific detail and is simple, impressionistic, and approximate. Whatever the memory, many children will have difficulty recalling details to represent. It is usually easier to draw an item or detailed process from observation than from memory. However, the data reduction involved in representing a memory can still serve the child and teacher well in reflecting the child's initial knowledge and experience with the topic of investigation.

Paradoxically, however, drawing from memory can help many young children articulate complex ideas. For example, in the first phase of a project on pets, one child drew two people, a car, and a cat in a box. He was able to explain the events depicted through his drawing. He described how the family cat was being taken to the vet for shots and his father asked him to come along and talk to the cat on the way to comfort it because it was usually unhappy in the car. The drawing greatly helped the teacher and child together to reconstruct the scene in words. This helped the child share his experience with the other children and write a suitable caption for his drawing. It is only when the details of such a story are clear that the teacher can gain insight into how much the child understands about the topic as a result of the experience.

Rich discussions occur when children are encouraged to share their experiences in detail. As the teacher invites children to explain the details of experiences represented in their drawings, she provides an active model of the careful and interested listener, asking questions for clarification when needed. This model helps the children learn to listen and to question each other in a similar way. The processes of oral sharing have also been described by Gallas (1994) as contributing to "the complex process that teachers go through to build a powerful, inclusive classroom community." This community-building in the classroom is an essential aspect of good project work. Our experience is that children talk about the topic of study among themselves in the classroom, at recess, after school, and at home with their parents because they are interested in it. The more details in drawings are discussed at "sharing times" in the classroom, the easier it is for the teacher to help the children identify and discuss areas of confusion or gaps in their understandings. These discussions then provide the basis for formulating questions for follow-up investigation.

The drawings completed in the early stages of a project represent children's prior understandings of the topic. Early drawings can be compared with the much more detailed ones achieved later in the study. Both teachers and children can appreciate the evidence of progress they have made in understanding various elements of the topic under investigation. A sequence of drawings completed at different times during the project can give children props or cues to help them discuss their learning in conferences with teacher and parents. An example of a sequence of drawings from observation of a car wheel by a 4-year-old girl involved in a project on cars is presented below (from Beneke, 1998), as well as other examples of sequences of drawings from observation by first graders involved in a project on bicycles that were made available by their teacher, Jolyn Blank.

Phase II: Developing the Project

In the second phase of the project, the children are extending and deepening their knowledge of the topic with a shared perspective from primary and secondary sources of information. During Phase II, their greater experience with real objects, events, processes, and roles is the major source of information for drawing. On field visits, the children make sketches to remind them later of what they have seen. Sketches focus children's attention at the field site and facilitate later discussion on return to the classroom. Children can use the sketches as bases for further illustrations of the phenomena being studied. Because of time constraints in the field, these sketches are usually drawn economically, including only the most salient and significant details. Field sketches involve looking closely at the objects and people studied and carefully selecting information to record about the parts of an object, the stages in a process, or the sequence of actions taken by a person.

Back in the classroom, the children can elaborate their drawings with reference to photographs and secondary sources of information. They can undertake sustained observational drawing of

Figure 7.1   A sequence of observational drawings of a wheel by a 4-year-old participating in a project on cars. Times 1, 2, and 3 were interspersed with tactile exploration and discussion. All three drawings were done on the same day

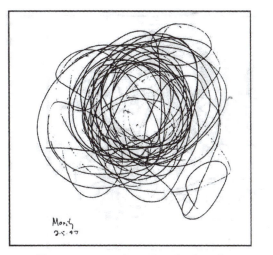

TIME 1

Source: Reprinted by permission from Beneke (1998).

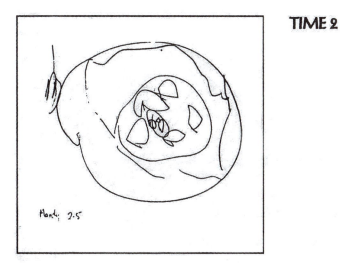

TIME 2

Source: Reprinted by permission from Beneke (1998).

(Continued)

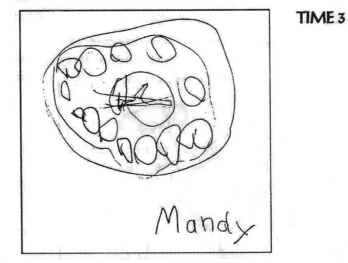

Source: Reprinted by permission from Beneke (1998).

Figure 7.2   A sequence of drawings of a bicycle by a first grader participating in a project on bicycles

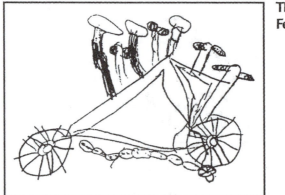

Source: Reprinted by permission from the Peoria School District, Peoria, Illinois.

(Continued)

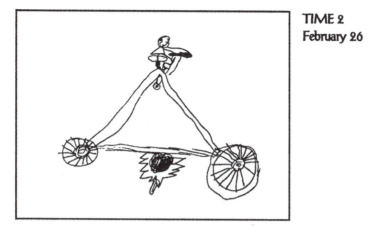

TIME 2
February 26

Source: Reprinted by permission from the Peoria School District, Peoria, Illinois.

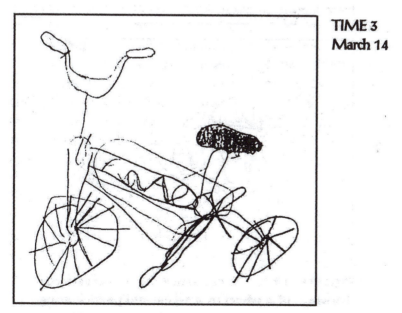

TIME 3
March 14

Source: Reprinted by permission from the Peoria School District, Peoria, Illinois.

Figure 7.3   Another sequence of drawings of a bicycle by a first grader participating in a project of bicycles

TIME 1
February 11

Source: Reprinted by permission from the Peoria School District, Peoria, Illinois.

TIME 2
February 26

Source: Reprinted by permission from the Peoria School District, Peoria, Illinois.

artifacts collected during Phase II. Increasingly detailed knowledge can be represented as it is collected. Sustained drawing enables children to study the nature of things, shapes, colors, textures, and other attributes. It encourages children to examine the relationship of parts to the whole of objects. "Close observation—mixed with wonder—is essential for the development of the artist, scientist, writer, as well as mathematician, humorist, inventor, and more" (Ruef, 1994, p. 22).

In a video, George Forman (1993) describes how his son, Jed, learns about how a bicycle works through the process of drawing it in detail. In turn, Jed talks about his drawing, revisits the bicycle itself, talks about what he observes, and resumes his drawing. By these means, Jed corrects his early impressions of how the pedal, chain, and wheels are connected and improves his understanding of how the bicycle moves. Another example shows how children themselves can appreciate the value of drawing to learn. A teacher in South Carolina told us about a kindergarten child who discovered for the first time that he could draw in the context of a project on the seashore. He developed a strong interest in crabs and drew many of them with increasing attention to detail. At the end of the project, the teacher was reviewing this boy's portfolio of project work. Looking at his drawings of crabs, she asked him to tell her about them. After a while, she exclaimed, "Sammy, how did you get to know so much about crabs?" Sammy replied, "Well, you see, the more I drew, the more I learned."

Processes and roles can be represented in an "event map," or in a drawing in which time and location are identified and labeled with words and measures. The sketches of the same object or event in the field made by several children can lead to animated discussion and argument about what was actually observed. In such cases, the teacher can encourage children's dispositions to be empirical by suggesting that they take opportunities to revisit the site or look again at the objects or photographs of them to verify the actual facts.

Interdisciplinary links can be facilitated as drawings and captions are prepared to enhance a composite representation such as a poster, a class museum exhibit, or book. Drawings can also be included in representations of phenomena prepared by a group. The drawings can often help to clarify the connections between different parts of the work contributed by the individual children within it. For example, in the development of a classroom museum, rocks and shells could be classified and labeled for display, their frequency counted and represented in a chart or graph, and the locations at which they were found could be mapped. Depending on the maturity of the children, the labels might include the age of the rocks, and timelines might be used to show their respective ages. Drawings could include the terrain in which different types of

Figure 7.4   Event Map by Hannah Hinchman

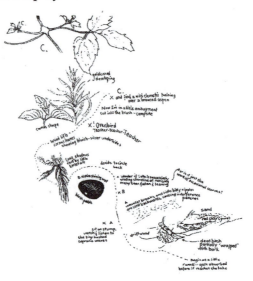

Source: Personal communication with Hannah Hinchman.

rocks were found, the shore location of different kinds of shells, and the location of the co-occurrence of different kinds of rocks or shells. Language and math skills can combine with social studies and science concepts and representations to enable the children to develop a sound, balanced understanding of the topic.

Multistage work such as the construction of a building or making a model village requires drawing for the processes of planning and drafting the evolution of the ideas as the work progresses. Field sketches can serve as the basis for such work. Other kinds of multistage work include presenting a dramatic performance with appropriate scenery; making a complex model of, for example, a farm, a factory, or a town; or making a simulation game featuring the main cause-and-effect relations associated with a topic.

Drawings of many different kinds can be included in project work. Sometimes a drawing can be simply executed at one sitting; at other times, it may be revisited and indeed, added to several times before it is complete. In the case of a revisited drawing, it may be of interest to the teacher as documentation of the progress made by a child or a group of them. Photocopies made at different times in the drawing process can record the progressive addition of detail leading to the finished product. Such documentation is helpful to other children interested in this kind of long term work.

Sometimes a drawing may stand alone with only a brief caption to indicate its significance to the study. At other times, there may be word labels added to a drawing indicating the technical terms for the parts of the object, time taken for processes depicted, or weights to indicate amounts of material shown, and so on. In project work there are many opportunities to mix media and means of communication to render a more accurate, detailed, and informative representation. As the children grow older, they can undertake increasingly complex combinations of representational strategies.

Most of the drawing in the second phase of a project is observational. However, it is important to note that younger children will mix observational drawing with memory or symbolic drawing, adding in figures or objects they would like to have represented there as well. For example, a group of five-year-olds drawing a bicycle in their classroom added drawings of the sun to their pictures and people riding the bicycles. To judge from the children's conversation at the time, the tendency to provide these additions was probably provoked by the power of their association of bicycles with the outdoors and being with other people. The difference between the quality of the drawing of the bicycles and the quality of the added information was considerable. The suns and added people tended to be more symbolic representations than realistic. For example, a typical circle with rays was used for the sun and primitive "hairpin" or "sausage" figures for the people, in sharp contrast to the more mature and informative drawing of the bicycles themselves.

Drawing from observation is informative for the child. Close observation leads the child to notice details and discover relationships. London (1989) writes about this kind of engagement:

We have the responsibility to see for ourselves and not to settle for hearsay. If we live our lives in rumor and hearsay, who we are and what we do will reflect not the world of our own experiences but the diluted, inaccurate reflections cast by others. Seeing something is to meet the thing.

Drawing can be further encouraged to increase analytical thinking. Throughout the range of different kinds of drawing, from drawings labeled with words to structural analyses labeled with short paragraphs and exploded drawings (drawings in which parts of an object are separated and enlarged), there are many ways for children to learn about the function of the parts of an object, the role of a person, the sequence of stages in a process, the layers in a cross-section, and so forth. Technical drawing of this kind is used in science text books, for example, in engineering or medicine, at any level of study in these subjects because words and numbers alone are insufficient for conveying detailed and complex information. Even where an entity is too small to see with a microscope, scientists still speculate about structure in drawings and three-dimensional models. Moline (1995) makes the point that

Reading and writing visual texts is not merely a transitional phase which is later discarded in favor of reading and writing words: visual text elements can be highly complex and are used extensively at all levels of learning through to university text books and post graduate research papers. Visual texts are therefore not an academically "soft option" to verbal texts, since they can be equally demanding to produce.

Drawing can also be decorative or sometimes abstract. It is helpful to have folders in which children can keep their individual pieces of project work, both for completed items and for those pieces that are still being worked on. The outside fronts and backs of these folders can be illustrated with pictures of items of particular interest to the children. Sometimes children's work can be specially featured on paper with illuminated borders made up of miniature drawings depicting details referred to in the text. This kind of drawing makes the material more memorable to the child as well as making the content of the work more accessible to other children. Illuminated borders are sometimes designed by teachers for children's work, but in the context of a project, the process of designing and making the border can itself be an important opportunity for the child to consolidate his or her own learning.

Creative written work such as poems or descriptive prose essays can sometimes benefit from an accompanying piece of art. This might involve the kind of drawing which is less informative or decorative than it is abstract and impressionistic. Such art might be primarily expressive of personal feelings or impressions rather than representing information.

Phase III: Concluding a Project

In the third phase of a project, most of the questions asked earlier in the study will have been answered in the course of field work or research with secondary sources of information. Although the time must come to bring the work of a project to a close, it is not because every question will have been answered and every research avenue exhausted. The reasons for finishing a project have more to do with other aspects of work to be included in the school year and the need to move on to other studies. In fact, it is important for children not to think that they know everything there is to know about a topic by the end of a project. On the contrary, from project work, children learn how the answer to any question provokes us to ask further questions at new levels of inquiry and understanding.

In the third phase of a project, some particularly interested children may want to speculate on what the answers to some of their new questions might be. An investigation of stores and markets today might give rise to questions about other kinds of buying and selling in the future. A study of rapid change over time lends itself naturally to speculation about the future. Predictions can be well expressed in speculative drawings. A study of a building, newspaper, or business may prompt designs of how things might look in a future time or other place.

At this time, the teacher can assess how well the children have learned the main ideas that emerged from the study of the topic. Planning for the culminating event to share the work with others can involve considerable discussion. This discussion will provide useful opportunities for review and evaluation of what has been accomplished. There are other opportunities for review involving drawing. The main information learned in the project can be applied by children in the design of a simulation in a board, track, or card game. The imaginative activity involved in such work helps children to personalize their new knowledge, making the project even more memorable.

Drawings, especially for the younger children, can be very helpful in enabling them to represent what they have learned in the course of the work in a way that others not involved can appreciate their experiences and efforts. In one kindergarten class, the children paired up with their 5th-grade buddies (ages 10–11) and shared three pictures they had selected from their project folders to explain what they had learned through their project work. The older children were to write what the young children told them about the items in the pictures. Elsewhere, in a first-grade class, the children were invited to draw and label as much as possible about what they had learned in a picture to present to others.

In summary, project work drawings may be of many different kinds: rough sketches, plans for future work, parts of larger composite pieces of work, or scenery for a dramatic presentation. A few drawings may be discarded, having served their purposes (like rough drafts or "scratch" notes). Many drawings will be intended for worthier final destinations, taking their place in a book or report, on a poster, or in the child's individual project folder. They may be given to informants in recognition and appreciation for their help or displayed in the library for others to learn from and enjoy. Above all, drawing for projects should be regarded as important school work, not taken home each day to disappear from the learning environment of the classroom. The third section of this chapter is devoted to discussion of strategies for the teacher to encourage purposeful drawing in the context of project work.

TEACHING STRATEGIES THAT ENCOURAGE DRAWING

The value placed on drawing is one of the characteristics of the culture of an early childhood or elementary classroom where projects are a regular part of the work. In this section, we address some of the issues teachers have raised with regard to encouraging drawing in their classrooms. These issues fall into three main categories: encouraging children to draw, building a drawing community in the classroom, and setting expectations and standards for children's drawing.

Encouraging Children to Draw

Teachers sometimes describe children as resistant to drawing and cite this observation as a reason not to insist upon it in their classrooms, perhaps because many children, by the age of five, assert that they cannot draw. However, teachers rarely, if ever, decline to teach or encourage reading on the grounds that the children in their class don't want to read. Our experience suggests that the desire to engage in almost any activity in a social setting is a function, to some extent, of cultural expectations. When children have the opportunity to observe respected peers or adults deeply engaged in an activity, it is likely to be valued by most children, and they will strive to engage in it themselves.

In the matter of reading, writing, and other academic subjects, evidence that a child dislikes required work is not a reason to omit it from the child's schedule. On the contrary, required tasks are insisted upon, and many teachers go to great lengths to make all required activities interesting and desirable to children. The same can apply to drawing.

Further evidence for the social origin of attitudes to drawing can be found in the response of many teachers to a child's apparent reluctance to draw as compared to his or her response to a child's reluctance to read. If a child in our culture complains because she "can't draw," the adult tends to offer sympathy and reassurance. The adult may say that he too cannot draw very well and that has not handicapped him too much in life. Sometimes the adult goes on to say drawing is one of those things that some people can do and others can't and that people are just born with or without the ability to draw. However, the adult's responses to young children who complain of not being able to read, for instance, are often quite different. They usually explain to such children that reading is very difficult, but you learn it gradually over a long time with lots of practice and help from the teacher and everyone around you, and that in time you will learn to read, just like everyone else. Younger children, those around age three, rarely resist drawing because they have not yet learned to believe that they cannot draw! Thus, it is a good idea to introduce purposeful drawing as early as young children wish to make marks on paper.

If drawing is to be perceived by children as valued in the culture of the classroom, the teacher must respond in similar ways to both children's reluctance to draw and their reluctance to read. Teachers must show children that they value drawing as an essential form of representation and show many examples of how drawings can enhance text, diagrams, or mathematical statements as well as express feelings.

Building a Drawing Community

One requirement of a classroom in which drawing is encouraged is that children be invited to explore the processes of drawing without fear of rebuke or ridicule when their efforts turn out to be less effective than they had intended. Drawing tends to be quite a public activity in a classroom. Unlike writing, drawing is more easily seen by others: it is hard to hide drawings you are working on. A gradually developing skillfulness in draughtsmanship thrives in a classroom culture in which drawing is a valued means of communication for all. Such a culture is appreciative of open communication, expressiveness, originality, and trial and error and honors children's intentions and the process of working on successive approximations towards their intended goal. Adults should resist the temptation to infer children's intentions and offer adult solutions to the drawing problems young children encounter. As Goodnow (1977) has noted in a report on her research on children's drawing, "The apparent disorder in children's behavior—its apparent lack of principles or rules—is due to our own ignorance of the principles they work by" (p. 60). Children must feel genuinely safe and free to make tentative and repeated attempts and to talk openly with others about their work.

Explicit Expectations

Creating a culture in the classroom that encourages drawing involves making clear how drawing is regarded by the adults and their expectations of children's attention to it. One basic characteristic of this culture would be the expectation that students would continuously be improving their drawing and using it to communicate what they are learning. An expectation at first grade (6–7 year-olds) and beyond would be that each child would draw at some time within the school day, in the way that writing is normally required every day. The drawing required for project work, however, would be different for each child, and not all of it is destined for sharing or public display.

The Classroom Environment

Making provision for daily drawing involves preparing space and time and real objects to draw. It also means teaching children to manage a variety of drawing materials, mark-making tools, paint, and paper. Children can be expected to select media and materials for their needs, prepare space in which to work, mix paint, clean up when their work is completed, and account in some way for how they have used their time and what they have accomplished. All project work involves children in managing transitions between different tasks, but drawing especially may involve some specific housekeeping strategies.

Through their management of the physical preparation for drawing activity, the children can learn respect for the tools and materials. The teacher takes responsibility for training the children, as appropriate for their age, on how to care for the materials by calm and persistent reminders and insistence on good practices. However, that insistence should be accompanied by the communication of values in respect of efficiency and economy. Scarce resources have to be safeguarded to avoid waste and ensure that they are maintained in good condition. Children can be particularly vigilant in developing a collective responsibility in areas of work for which they have a personal appreciation.

Noncompetitive Climate

Some classroom climates, intentionally or not, encourage children to be competitive and to compare their work to that of others. Such comparisons do not help the development of a community culture that encourages drawing. Take, for example, the common practice of putting artwork depicting the same objects or ideas by every child on a bulletin board or in the hallway. When every child's work on the same subject is displayed, each product can be compared with every other one. This means that a few children may judge—sometimes correctly—that their work is less "good" than that of most other children. In order to avoid such disparaging comparisons, teachers have resorted to giving instructions to ensure that every child can achieve the same standard. The consequence can often result in a sacrifice of individuality for the sake of uniformity.

Standardizing work products is inappropriate and irrelevant for project work. For example, informative drawing is an especially valuable means of representation precisely because it enables children to show a personal perspective that can enrich everyone's interest in the topic. In a project, so many different kinds of drawing can represent interdependent findings about the topic; there will be no "class sets" of the same work to display. Instead, each final draft picture can make a unique contribution to some part of the project work. Taken together, the different findings help to explain how a bicycle moves and what parts it needs to have in order to work.

CHOOSING APPROPRIATE LEVELS OF CHALLENGE

Group discussion of the demands of various drawing tasks and activities—sketching, drafting, elaborating, and so on—help children to elect to draw at different levels of formality and complexity. One child may want to contribute a drawing for the cover of a class book; another, a drawing to be included in the book; and yet another may rarely volunteer to make drawings available for public display. These preferences for the final destination of drawings can be respected without negative effects on any child's progress in developing his or her drawing skill. If every child is expected to draw every day, every child is likely to make progress, albeit at different rates and at different levels. As even the child who is least competent at drawing gains confidence, the whole class can expect to develop considerable facility in representational drawing.

Exercising Choice in Drawing

Opportunity to make choices can often improve children's motivation to participate in an activity. Children can choose media and subject matter when it comes to drawing. They can also choose among many different kinds of drawing in project work. In addition, they can take on levels of challenge in their drawing that are appropriate to their current levels of achievement. The choice of level of challenge particularly facilitates the development of self-assessment strategies and understandings about the demands of particular kinds of drawing. In some classrooms, suggestions are made by the teacher to invite drawings for a specific display, scenery for a play, or for a poster or game. These may be requested over several days. In that time, the children come to understand the complexities of the task. Consider the following example:

In one classroom where checkered flags were required for a play, the teacher invited the children to paint these over the course of a week. Eight children in a class of 30 responded to this challenge. The first flags were painted by children to whom the idea had immediate appeal and who were not afraid to work with little direction as to the form of the finished product. By the third day, the discussions of the first drawings had generated some key information about the nature of a checker pattern. Those children who subsequently undertook this painting task were able to build into their work an appreciation of the "horizontal and vertical," the "equidistant parallel lines," and the "black and white squares," which "touched at the corners" in parts of the rather impressionistic flags completed earlier. The problem solving became increasingly sophisticated with each day's discussion throughout the week. Children who completed flags earlier also had a chance to paint another flag if they wished.

SETTING EXPECTATIONS AND STANDARDS FOR CHILDREN'S DRAWING

It is likely that children become aware that the teacher values drawing when it is clear that it is expected as a regular and significant part of their project work. Both explicit expectations and the support and encouragement of the community culture in the classroom are important if confident drawing is to become part of every child's project work. We now discuss the strategies teachers can use to help children develop their drawing skills. This is important because children gain confidence in their ability to draw when they experience success in developing their own competence in graphic representation.

Becoming a Teacher Who Draws

Unfortunately, many teachers have little confidence in their abilities to help children to improve their drawing. Indeed, many teachers in the North American culture do not themselves draw or use the activity of drawing in their own lives. For those in this position, we recommend Edwards' book *Drawing on the Right Side of the Brain* (1979) or Hannah Hinchman's *A Life in Hand* (1991) and *A Trail through Leaves* (1997). However, even if you do not draw or have not done so for a very long time, but you want to help children to develop their drawing skills, there are several ways to do so without a great deal of specialist knowledge of art education, desirable though this may be.

Peer Modeling

Much can be accomplished through peer modeling, where children learn from each other. The impulse to draw is likely to flourish in a classroom where a variety of examples of drawings done by peers are on display on bulletin boards or available in class book collections. Peer modeling is a particularly powerful influence on children's drawing when work products are discussed by children and with the teacher in the class group. The work is most usefully selected by the teacher for the purpose of discussing drawing strategies and effects. In the brief discussion of the positive features of a few drawings each day, much can be done to sensitize the children to the advantages of different techniques.

A Language to Talk about Drawing

Children can draw thoughtfully and intentionally when they work in an environment where words are frequently used to describe different kinds of visual images and graphic effects. In the early childhood classroom, for example, there are many opportunities to talk about the kinds of illustrations found in children's books. For younger children, the illustrations are often more accessible aids to understanding the stories than the text. Children can acquire through such talk a vocabulary for describing line, shape, color, tone, value, and texture.

In addition to words used to describe particular effects in finished drawings, there are words that can be used to describe the techniques and strategies for achieving those effects. Children themselves can share successes and challenges arising in their use of particular techniques. Skillful drawing involves the development of abilities. Discussion of techniques should be straightforward, direct, matter-of-fact, and open. Teachers can add their own suggestions if familiar with the issues discussed. There is no need for the reverence or mystique that sometimes obscures discussions about young children's "art." No more place needs to be accorded self-deprecation or self-aggrandizement in the discussion of drawing than there would be in discussions of writing or math skills.

The description of drawing conveyed above may suggest that there are sub-skills to be learned similar to those for writing and math. However, we think it is important to recognize some essential differences between conventional academic skills and the representational skills involved in drawing. The purpose is not that children should develop a convergent style in drawing such as they would in writing or computation. Rather, the variety of possibilities for drawing can open up ways for children to explore and develop their drawing ability on a daily basis as part of life in the classroom. With these differences in mind, there are at least three messages to be conveyed by the teacher to help children willingly strive to improve their drawing.

The first message concerns the value of originality in drawing. Originality, difference, and variety are to be valued in drawing. Originality is usually achieved quite easily when children draw freehand. It is to be expected that different children may have different thoughts to convey in their drawings. These differences can be explored in discussions children have about the subject of their drawing and the processes of freehand drawing.

In respect of the value of originality, then, it is important to caution against the use of templates, stencils, tracing, or coloring in pre-drawn outlines, which can suggest the opposite value. The use of these techniques implies that there is a right way to draw, and some intermediary object between the brain and the fingers can enable you to "do it right" (i.e., like everyone else who uses the same object). Using such "aids" is actually more difficult for young children than freehand drawing. Some teachers mistakenly believe they are helping children through these intermediary objects and gadgets. In fact, training children to use them can seriously inhibit the development of freehand drawing skills. These convergent production techniques intervene between intentional thought and mark making, between the intention to represent in drawing and the freehand drawing process itself.

The second message to be conveyed to children is that they will inevitably find themselves at very different levels of competence in drawing compared with others in the class. This is an important message to combine with the earlier expectation that they will progress beyond their current level of ability in the direction of greater competence. Whatever level of competence children may judge themselves to have, they will nonetheless all be equally able to contribute to any group discussion of representation in drawing. Some more primitive levels of technique have particular understandings to convey about the nature of objects or processes. Children are helped when they come to see that there is no intrinsic value in any one kind of drawing as compared with another kind, for example, the execution of a simple line drawing compared with a detailed rendering of a tree with every leaf drawn on every twig. The decision between these alternatives would depend on the visual information or sensation that the person doing the drawing wanted to represent.

The third message to give children concerns cultural conventions. For instance, there is a convention that the distant background of a scene should be portrayed behind the main items in the foreground; the sky should come down to meet the ground at the horizon in the picture rather than be represented as a blue bar at the top and a green bar at the bottom of the picture. Such conventions can be seen for what they are: cultural conventions. They need not be suggested to children who show no desire to explore the advantages of those conventions for themselves. Especially damaging to some children's drawing development can be the rote learning of "how to draw" particular objects such as dogs or houses. Hinchman (1997) tells how she learned to draw horses from a book as a child. She describes how this continues to have an inhibiting effect on her drawing of the horses she can see from the windows of her home. Teachers can best encourage children in their drawing if they can recognize the intrinsic merit in any form of representation young children choose for themselves. Their choices will be made on the basis of their appreciation of pictures drawn by others, adults or children. Dissatisfaction with his or her own level of skill when expressed by a child can be countered with suggestions of alternative strategies to try out or other children with whom to talk to seek advice and assistance.

These three ideas can help teachers to encourage successive attempts by children to apply their drawing skills to exploring alternative effects in the representation of people, objects, events, or processes of interest to themselves and to their classmates.

SUMMARY

In the context of a project, children can be encouraged and supported in their desire to find out about the world around them. We suggest that drawing can offer children an especially valuable and satisfying means of investigating and representing important features of a topic of study. There are opportunities for children to engage in many different kinds of drawing for a variety of different purposes. Drawing provides for a wide range of individual ideas to be shared, and project work thrives on the consideration of a rich body of information about a topic. Finally, it is important for teachers to be confident in their encouragement and support of children as they develop their ability to draw. Through their own confidence, teachers can inspire children to enliven and personalize their project work with drawing and thereby achieve the appropriate depth of learning.

EIGHT

Projects with Younger Children

INTRODUCTION

Teachers often wonder at what age children can begin doing project work. Considering that from birth, children have a profound sense of wonder, an innate drive for exploration, and an emerging intellectual capacity, we hear of teachers introducing projects to children from infancy. This is the case, for example, in the infant–toddler centers of Reggio Emilia in Italy. In this chapter, however, we will discuss aspects to be considered when involving toddlers from 18 to 36 months of age and preschoolers ages 4 and 5 in projects. This chapter describes what project work looks like in early childhood classrooms and will provide examples from our direct experience with teachers and young children.

THE BENEFITS OF PROJECT WORK FOR YOUNG LEARNERS

Young children benefit from doing project work, as it provides opportunities for them to unlock their potential by taking initiative, pursuing their interests, working collaboratively, and becoming self-directed learners. Preschool teachers have found that when toddlers have had exposure to certain aspects of project work, they are better prepared to embrace it when they are older. Having had previous experience with projects, these children are increasingly more likely to come to projects with an openness to novelty, confidence in their ability to explore the world around them, and readiness to engage with others, teachers and peers, as they make their discoveries. Similarly, teachers of the older children have found that youngsters entering the elementary grades who have done project work for several previous years are usually better able to apply and test their knowledge through methodical inquiry and verification. They have become more capable than their less-experienced peers at formulating questions, brainstorming ideas to make topic webs, utilizing tools for exploration, and using a wide variety of materials and representational strategies to show their deepening understanding of the project topics.

When we began our work with toddlers, there was some uncertainty about what project activity toddlers might benefit from. The teachers in our school decided to focus on the following: encouraging curiosity, offering opportunities to explore the physical world through the senses, using vocabulary associated with discovery, and taking pleasure in representing their ideas using a variety of media. We began calling our work with the youngest children "project practice." In this way, we avoided having unrealistic expectations and felt free to explore project work that was developmentally appropriate for the age of the children involved. It is important to note here that, following careful documentation of the children's responses over the project timeline, it became apparent that "practice" was not an accurate term to describe the work we were observing in front of us. Given that the word "practice" sometimes brings with it connotations of preparation for some future competencies and that we were able to observe the intrinsic value the project work was having for the toddlers in real time, we determined that "project experience" was actually the more accurate term to describe what the children were experiencing. This is an important distinction to make, as it highlights continuity and discovery of learning that project work can provide for both teachers and children.

Parents also comment that the early project work has an impact on how children approach experiences outside school, as they frequently want to carry on with investigating more about the topics they are studying in school whenever they get a chance. Parents perceive their children strengthening their inborn dispositions to investigate that are developed through project work (as discussed in chapter 1). Parents also feel more connected to their children's school life, as the youngsters often talk about what they are investigating and learning. They indicate that they want to take books or other items from home that can contribute to the collective learning of their class and to enrich the study of the topic. For example, during a study of bones in a classroom of 5-year-olds, one child brought in chicken bones, another an air-cast that had been worn by his father and a pair of crutches, and several contributed by bringing X-rays from their homes and putting together a collection of items that showed different bones in the body.

WHICH TOPICS ARE MEANINGFUL FOR CHILDREN TO EXPLORE IN THE EARLY YEARS?

Topics for young children need to be about phenomena within their own experience in order for them to be meaningful, build on their prior knowledge, and allow for them to construct new understandings. When selecting a topic for this age group, the criteria addressed in chapter 3 are relevant together with a few additional considerations. These are particularly concerned with ways to build on younger children's current interests and increase the relevance of the project experiences to them.

Topics for Toddlers

Among the topics most valuable to toddlers are those that relate to aspects of their daily lives and that can build on previous knowledge and firsthand experiences. When investigating familiar objects, events, locations, routines, and people, toddlers can become more confident and increasingly take initiative in pursuing their investigations. There is so much in toddlers' personal environments about which they can deepen their understanding and make better sense of their world that there are ample possibilities for study. Project topics for this age group might include learning about oneself, food, pets, water, places and people at school, clothing, plants, and many others.

Good topics for toddlers may also include those that enable them to explore cause—effect relationships. Toddlers are drawn to the effect of their actions on objects and on people nearby. These topics offer ways for toddlers to understand that certain actions bring about predictable responses and reactions. A study of sounds would be an example of a topic that involves causation. As children interact with different objects, they can listen to the sounds they make, for instance, banging on a drum, sliding their fingers over the strings of a guitar, knocking on a door or ringing a doorbell. Another topic that is rich in cause and effect possibilities can be a study of balls. Here toddlers explore the impact of their own force and motion and how these affect the movement and the trajectory of different balls; some roll, some bounce, some are easier to throw, and others to kick (See Katz, 1999).

Topics that provide toddlers the opportunities to organize objects by their characteristics and identify similarities, differences, and associations can also attract their interest and enable them to create and analyze general relationships, promoting the development of their reasoning skills. A study of fruits could enable children to sort and group them by color, texture, size, shape, and/or taste. It would also help them understand that most fruits are different on the outside from on the inside, that some need to be peeled, that some can be used to produce juice, and that all of them have seeds. This knowledge can be useful for choosing and handling different fruits and in helping to prepare snacks or meals.

Topics that help children to understand how people interact with and relate to one another and to become aware of the roles people have as members of a group are worthy of young children to learn about. For instance, they could learn about what the people they interact with daily at school do (e.g., the classroom teacher, the music teacher, the nurse, the librarian, cook, janitor, bus driver, etc.).

Other worthwhile topics for toddlers may include a study of their own bodies. In this case, they can learn about different body parts and what they can do with them (e.g., "You use your legs to walk or run, your eyes to see, your ears to hear," etc.). Moreover, they could also conduct a study on how they have changed from when they were babies: the differences and similarities in their physical characteristics and things they are able to do.

Topics for project work with such young children must always allow for rich sensory exploration, as this is how they are most likely to acquire useful firsthand information; in addition, it is also important to understand that the experience of what we refer to as "fieldwork" is as valuable to toddlers as it is to older children. However, in view of the fact that it might sometimes be difficult to take toddlers and preschoolers to field sites that are far away, it is helpful to select topics that will allow them to conduct fieldwork in their immediate surroundings. These sites may include places in the school campus as well as in its vicinity.

Topics for Preschool-Age Children

Topics selected for preschoolers may be different from those a teacher would select for toddlers. Even though preschoolers still benefit from learning about aspects of their daily lives, topics that relate to familiar places, processes, and objects within their occasional experience can also be introduced to help them understand how things in their world work. These could include: studying a nearby restaurant, the hospital, the construction site, going shopping, the school bus, various homes, chairs, pizza, signs, and the school's neighborhood, among many others. The following examples describe experiences of topics studied in preschool classrooms.

A class of 4-year-olds set out to study the process of making bread. After connecting with their prior experiences about the topic, the children wanted to know how bread was made. They made predictions about the ingredients needed and the process of preparation:

"You put Tuna fish in a bowl and mix it with flour. Next, you add water and milk. You mix and mix, and then you put it in a frying pan and after waiting and waiting, you will get a loaf of bread."

The children had the opportunity to test their predictions through experimentation and concluded that the result did not look, smell, or taste like bread. But after several weeks of their repeated experiences with experts, where they had the opportunity to ask questions, watch them making bread, and participate in the process, the children were able to begin to understand the effect of chemical reactions on matter—in this case, how different substances are mixed and cooked to make bread.

A group of 5-year-olds conducted a study of hotels. Most of the children in this class had traveled several times and had the experience of staying at a hotel. Nonetheless, they did not necessarily understand how hotels work: the roles of different staff members, the rationale for why different uniforms are worn within the same establishment, the variations in room features according to price, and that there is a process you need to go through when you arrive and depart from a hotel. The in-depth study of this topic helped the children understand the roles of different workers, the equipment and tools they use for their jobs, and the processes guests need to go through when staying at a hotel. This project could be useful to children when they travel and stay at a hotel in the future.

It is useful to note that topics for both toddlers and preschoolers can also add value to addressing developmentally appropriate learning expectations and outcomes (standards and benchmarks) as outlined by programs, states, or countries. Specifically, projects can provide children with opportunities to apply their growing skills in the context of real life. Worthwhile and age-appropriate project topics should give children the opportunity to do the following:

- learn and use new specialized vocabulary to describe familiar places, people, things, and events;
- listen to descriptions of experiences that are being shared during discussion among the children or by experts;
- pose questions and listen to the ideas of others;
- contribute to class discussion;
- classify objects according to one or more attributes;
- identify similarities and differences between objects;
- count items, use nonstandard units to measure objects and quantity, and develop and apply numeracy and literacy skills.

Some project topics could be selected for both the younger and older children, taking into account their levels of maturity, their interests, and the way they perceive the world. For instance, older children learning about their school may choose to study the school's transportation office, for example, the routes taken by the school buses and the schedules they need to follow in order to arrive at school on time. Toddlers, on the other hand, may conduct a study of how to get from their classroom to the different places in their school building, such as the music room, the playground, and the bathroom.

Although teachers of the younger children usually select the topic to be studied, they can be attentive and responsive to the children's interests and levels of maturity. Some of the topics chosen for these age groups might result in good project experiences, and some might not. Teachers need to explore and investigate topics in order to plan meaningful and age-appropriate experiences that will enable children to better understand their world.

DURATION OF PROJECTS FOR TODDLERS AND PRESCHOOLERS

Teachers of toddlers usually conduct projects that do not last as long as those carried out by older children. Toddlers undertake investigations that can last a few days (mini-projects) or up to a few weeks. Teachers of toddlers can also set up experiences of some features of a project before embarking on a full project. For example, since many children in the class were being toilet trained or soon would be, one teacher decided to hold a discussion about who used the toilet. Children began telling stories about their experiences; some shared that they used the toilet, and others said they didn't but that their older siblings did. She held this conversation with the children in preparation for a site visit to the school's bathroom to look at the objects that were there and how they worked. The youngsters had an opportunity to flush the toilet, listen to the sound of the water and observe its movement, and learn how to fasten and unfasten a roll of toilet paper from its fixture on the wall. The children also looked inside the water tank and washed their hands. As children were handling the different objects they saw, the teacher used specialized vocabulary associated with the experience: "You used the handle to flush the toilet, and the water inside the bowl went round and round." Once in the classroom, the teacher led a discussion about things the youngsters saw and did at the field site. She

Figure 8.1   Taking a close look at a fountain and making a field sketch

Source: Courtesy of teachers of Eton School in Mexico City.

prompted it by showing pictures she had taken during the visit so that the youngsters could revisit the experience. It is clear from this example that children were involved in discussion, fieldwork, and investigation, three important features of the project approach.

Preschool children can usually remain interested in a topic for a longer period of time than toddlers can, since their understanding of the world leads more easily to inquiries of greater depth. Their investigations to find answers to their questions might involve going on several field visits and consulting relevant experts on numerous occasions. Their level of maturity and confidence in their abilities to use various materials engages them in representing their learning in diverse ways, and the process of representation might take place over the course of several weeks.

One class of 5-year-olds conducted a study of fountains. After talking about them and making drawings of ones they had seen, they visited several places in the city to see different kinds of fountains. During the site visits, they had the opportunity to take a close look at the mechanisms needed for fountains to function and to talk to experts who explained how water pumps worked. The children had wondered about the following: "How does water get to a fountain?" "What does the inside of the motor look like?" and "How does the motor work?" Back in the classroom, some children were interested in how water pumps worked and made drawings and models to represent what they learned. Others made paintings of the different fountains they saw around the city and wrote signs for each of the fountains they depicted so that peers and other visitors could identify them. Next, a few children suggested to the teacher that they would like to build a fountain at school. The rest of the youngsters in the class were very excited about this idea, and the class decided to ask the principal's permission for this venture.

Once they received a positive response to their request, the children started working steadily to reach their objective. They first invited an architect to explain all of the things they would need to do and buy. After the expert's visit, they looked for a place in the school's campus near the water and electricity sources that would be needed in order for the fountain to function. Next, a small group of children made a detailed drawing of the design and a diagram that included measurements and explained how the fountain would work. Then they calculated the costs that building the fountain would involve by finding out and adding up the prices of the different materials they would use. Once the principal approved the design and the budget, the children started building their fountain with the help of the school's maintenance staff. They mixed cement with water, laid bricks, pasted pieces of tile on a wall to make their design, and helped the staff install the water pump and the Plexiglas pipes through which the water would run. The children's engagement and interest persisted over the course of 10 weeks, until they witnessed the completion of their work. The fountain has now become a landmark in the school that peers and adults enjoy visiting.

Projects can last a few days, a few weeks, or even months. Teachers can assess the duration of a project by considering if children have completed the following: (a) answered most of the questions they set out to investigate, (b) visited field sites and/or invited experts, (c) engaged in a wide variety of representations, or (d) lost interest in the topic of study.

Figure 8.2   Initial design of the fountain the children would build at school

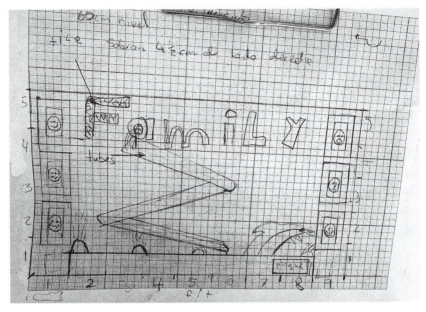

Source: Courtesy of teachers of Eton School in Mexico City.

Figure 8.3   Building the fountain

Source: Courtesy of teachers of Eton School in Mexico City.

Figure 8.4   The fountain has become a landmark of the school, which children and adults enjoy visiting

Source: Courtesy of teachers of Eton School in Mexico City.

PHASE I: HOW DO YOU START A PROJECT?

Teachers may start a project in different ways. In the Reggio Emilia preschools, some ways of starting a project involve what are called "provocations." In these cases, the teacher provokes the children to think about the topic and talk about it from the outset. Here are some suggestions that have worked well.

Teachers can begin by setting out familiar objects to engage the interest of young children. These are particularly effective when items are arranged in such a way as to remind children of their prior knowledge. As they interact with the objects that are likely to reveal their interests, wonderings, prior knowledge, and any misconceptions they may have about the topic, the teacher can learn about these by closely observing the children's actions and reactions, by listening to their spontaneous comments, or by joining in the conversation. The teachers can interpret the documentation they collect during these sessions in order to plan opportunities that will enable children to further explore their current understanding of a topic.

Objects that work well to start off a project are those that children are able to interact with. Teachers can note how the children observe and sometimes comment on the effects of their actions on the objects. Youngsters can also derive much satisfaction from arrangements of objects that invite them to put things together or move them around to rearrange them. These activities lead to sorting and grouping objects. Children's natural sense of wonder and curiosity drives them to ask questions about their experience with these items. The teacher can give words to the younger children to help them to seek answers to their questions. They learn by becoming actively involved in direct explorations of real objects and natural occurrences, which prompt them to observe, question, predict, and form conclusions. Consider the following example:

A teacher of two-year-olds set out to engage the children in a project on sounds. To provoke the children's interest, she used a pencil and started tapping it on an empty tin can. In the middle of the circle, she had set out different "drum-like" objects (an empty glass jar, a tin can, a wooden container, a plastic container, a metal pot, and a clay pot), as well as different "stick-like" objects (a pencil, a plastic spoon, a ladle, a straw and a paint brush). After watching her continue to tap on the tin can for a while, the children started to do the same with the different objects she had placed in the circle. Once the children were engaged in interacting with the diverse items, she began to document what she observed and heard. A child exclaimed, "This doesn't work!" when he took the straw and banged it on the wooden container. Another child said, "Mine is loud" as he stroked the ladle on the metal pot. Other children started making similar comments about the kinds of sounds being produced from the materials they chose. Becoming frustrated, the child who had picked the straw to tap on the wooden container chose a paintbrush and tried it out. "This one works," he said. Following his initiative, other children started changing the materials they were using.

After analyzing her documentation of the experience, the teacher identified the following questions for the children's research:

1. How can you make different sounds?
2. What kinds of sounds do different objects make?

With toddlers, it can be especially helpful to repeat the same provocation several times, to observe how they interact with the same objects on different occasions, and to identify further possibilities to guide the investigation of the topic. In the case of the objects to investigate sounds, the children discovered the different materials the objects were made of made a difference to the sounds they made. With the teacher's guidance, they began to distinguish the words used in their discussion: loud and soft, high and low, wood, metal and paper, thick and thin, and so on.

As children grow older, they have more understanding of how things work and can show what they already know in the way they interact with the provocation. A class of three- and four-year olds set out to conduct a study of plants. To begin the project and engage the children's interest, the teacher placed a clear plastic tub that contained a small amount of water on a table. Inside the container were pots with flowering plants and containers, which floated in the water. The teacher invited a small group of children to look at the items that she had arranged for the exploration. Some of them commented on what they saw: "I like flowers," "I have some purple flowers in my house that look like these," "There is water," and "Plants need water."

After a couple of minutes, the children started interacting with the objects. Some put their hands inside the tub to touch the water, others touched the leaves of the plants, and others used the containers to water the plants. It was interesting to see that the children watered the plants by pouring water on top of the flowers and leaves. As this took place, the teacher took notes of the children's conversations and photographs to document what happened. She repeated this experience with other small groups of children in her class so that all of them could interact with the provocation. After looking at the photographs she took during the sessions and reading her notes, she concluded that most children in her class had some prior knowledge of plants; they used some specialized vocabulary to talk about the parts of plants and mentioned other places where they had seen similar ones. She also recognized that most had misconceptions about how plants were watered, and she predicted that they probably did not know that water must be placed on the soil below to water the roots. The teacher clearly identified opportunities to plan further experiences

Figure 8.5   A child showing a misconception about how plants are watered

Source: Courtesy of teachers of Eton School in Mexico City.

so that children could gain greater understanding about these living organisms.

A project with preschool children can also begin with the exchange of personal stories in relation to a topic prompted by a familiar object, a photograph, a happening, or a story told by the teacher or a classmate. Preschoolers can represent these through dramatic play and through drawings, models, and paintings.

After having had the opportunity to connect with their prior knowledge through different kinds of provocations, many preschool children who have had previous experience of doing project work are able, with the guidance of their teacher, to formulate questions for investigation.

One day, the teacher of a class of four year-olds arrived late for school. As she rushed into the room, the children wanted to know what had happened to make her late. The teacher said, "My car broke down! I am not sure what happened to it. Some people who stopped to help me said it was the battery; others said there was probably something wrong with the engine. I waited until a tow truck came and took it to a repair shop where it will be fixed." The children started asking many questions: "Are cars' batteries the same as the ones I use for my toys?" "How does a car engine work?" "Why do cars break down?" "How do people fix cars?" and "Who works at a car repair shop?" Some also told stories about their experiences: "One day, when my dad was driving me to school, our car broke down. It was very near the school, so we got out and walked." As the teacher reflected upon her conversation with the children, the interest they showed, the questions they raised, and the stories they told, she decided to pursue an in-depth study of cars with her class.

Preschool teachers can also introduce children to making a topic web by guiding them through the process. The teacher may start by using key words from children's personal stories. In the case of a project on parks, the children may have told stories about trees, picnic tables, swings, flowers, grass, children, workmen, dogs, and so on. With the teacher's guidance, they can sort these words collectively into categories. This work might be done by the teacher with a small group of children who are already beginning to read. The categories might include plants, things to play on, people, and so on. These headings can be spaced out on a large piece of chart paper with room for small drawings to be posted in the appropriate categories.

Since most of these youngsters may not yet be able to write, their topic web would contain many more drawings than words. For example, each day more words may be used in personal stories about park experiences during the first phase of the study. These items can be drawn by the children on sticky notes and posted in the appropriate category on the chart. Drawings and words can be added to the web as the work continues. This can help focus the children's attention on the new vocabulary words they are learning throughout the project. Once the children become used to the format offered by a vocabulary web, they can refer to it in talking about different subtopics and areas of investigation in the project.

Figure 8.6   A topic web made by 5-year-old children with the guidance of their teacher

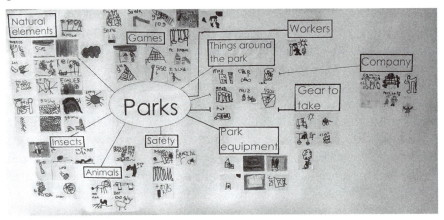

Source: Courtesy of teachers of Eton School in Mexico City.

PHASE II: CONDUCTING FIELD WORK AND INVITING EXPERTS TO VISIT

In the second phase of a project, children begin to seek answers to the questions that were identified or formulated in Phase I. Field work is important for young learners, as they rely more heavily on direct observation and sensory exploration than on secondary sources to get information. They are as acutely interested and engaged as older children during a field visit, and they gain new knowledge from what they see, touch, taste, smell, and hear.

Preparation for a Site Visit

Teachers of the younger children have found it important to plan the site visit carefully, as there are several considerations of elements that can help make field trips and site visits productive.

By way of example, teachers also need to consider the distance from the school to the field site; since it is challenging to transport toddlers in vehicles and take all precautions necessary to care for them, these visits could take place inside the school or within walking distance of the school. Preschoolers could go farther away, but they too might tire easily, get hungry, or need to use the bathroom during long bus rides.

It is a good idea also for teachers to inspect the field site before taking the children there to prevent frustrating situations that might not fulfill their expectations and that might be unsafe. For instance, a class of four-year-olds once visited an ice-cream factory. They were only allowed to look from a distance at the equipment and at the people who were working there. They were asked to stand under a window to watch, but none of them was tall enough to be able to see what was going on.

Good places for visits usually include small establishments or other places where people will allow children to look closely at things, to take field notes, and to ask questions. For example, a class of four-year-olds visited a bicycle repair shop, where the owner told them what different parts of the bicycles were called and explained how they worked. Next, he showed them how to pump air into the tires and how to screw bolts and nuts to put parts together. He then invited the children to try out what he had demonstrated. The youngsters also had time to take field notes and ask many questions.

Teachers of young children usually need to take several additional accompanying adults with them on trips. It could be valuable for teachers to meet with them prior to the trip to give them instructions about to how they can be helpful to the children in carrying out activities and in documenting the experience. A teacher of five-year-old children, who would be taking a trip to the botanical garden, called in the accompanying parents a few days before the trip. She explained where they would be going and communicated the purpose of the visit. Next, she gave each of the six accompanying adults a slip of paper with specific details of what they would do and the schedule they needed to follow. The text on the written note read as follows:

Dear Mrs._____,

I am excited about our upcoming visit, and I am grateful that you will be able to accompany us. I ask for your help with the following:

- *Please be at school at 9:00 a.m. sharp, since the bus will be leaving at 9:15 a.m.*

- *You will be taking care of and working with: _____, _____, and_____.*
- *Make sure to take: clipboards for the children in your group, small bags to collect samples, a pad where you can take notes of their conversations, and your camera.*
- *When we get to the botanical garden, the whole class will go together on a tour.*
- *After the tour, you and the children in your group will go the area called* fantastic forest *to take a close look at the trees. Encourage the children to make field sketches and to take notes of things that draw their attention. Collect samples of leaves of different trees if you find some on the ground.*
- *While the children are working, take notes of their conversations and comments. I know children posing and smiling at the camera can be irresistible, but I ask that you take photographs of children while they are exploring and taking notes.*
- *We will meet at the exit at 12:00 p.m. sharp to board the bus and return to school.*

I thank you for your enthusiasm and support,
Ms._____

Before the visit, teachers can take a look at the children's questions, decide which could be addressed and answered during the visit, and encourage the youngsters to make predictions about the answers. A simple chart can be used to record the questions and predictions so that these can be revisited upon returning to the classroom.

During the Field Visit

Young children may conduct a wide variety of activities at the site to further their knowledge about a topic. These could include talking to experts, watching processes, observing people at work, and taking a close look at machinery and equipment. Youngsters may also take tools on their trip to collect data. For example, they could take magnifying glasses to take a closer look at things, small bags to

Table 8.1 Questions-Predictions-Findings Chart

QUESTIONS	PREDICTIONS	FINDINGS	HOW WE FOUND THE INFORMATION
Are cacti plants?	No, because they don't have leaves.	Yes, they are plants.	We saw different species of cacti in the botanical gardens. Everything they have there are plants.
Do all plants have flowers?	No, because my grandma has a tree in her garden that doesn't have flowers.	Not all plants have flowers.	We were able to see many plants in the botanical gardens that don't have flowers.
Do all plants grow on the ground?	Yes, because they need soil to live.	No, there are some plants that live in water.	We were able to see the Water lily pond and saw the roots of the plants inside the water, and there was no soil.
Are plants babies first, then mommies and daddies, then grandparents, and then die?	Yes, because we saw a chili plant in Ms. Carmen's office that had baby chilies that were small and green, mommy and daddy chilies that were big and orange, and grannie chilies that were all wrinkled.	Yes, plants have a life cycle. They are born, they grow, and they die.	We asked an expert at the botanical gardens, and he explained about the life cycle of plants.
Are all animals good to plants, and that is why we see them around plants?	Yes, animals are good to plants and love them. That is why they live together with them.	Some animals, like earthworms, help plants to grow. Others are pests that damage plants.	The expert at the botanical garden told us that when we see animals too close to plants, it doesn't always mean that they are friends. Many animals just want to eat the plants.

collect samples of objects they see at the site or along the way, small-scale clipboards, pieces of paper, and pencils to record information and help them remember things that caught their attention.

Upon arrival at the site, it is usually helpful to take a tour together as a whole. Then the teacher may choose to divide the children into smaller groups to carry out activities that address their particular interests. Some could conduct interviews, others could watch people at work, and others could sketch objects of interest, while the rest could look at tools and equipment. Among other activities children may do at a site, they usually take notes and make field sketches of things that catch their attention in order to bring back information to the classroom.

When toddlers make field sketches, they do not usually reflect aspects of their experiences at the site accurately. For example, one group of toddlers visited a beauty salon located near to their school. While sketching, the adults approached them, looked at their scribbles, and asked questions. One of the children answered, "This is the chair for people who come here." Another one said, "This is the person cutting hair," and a third one said, "I am drawing a hen." Some others were not able to tell the adults about their sketches, since they were not yet able to express their ideas in words. The children in this class clearly showed different levels of skillfulness. Nonetheless, most of them were interested and engaged in the investigation.

It might sometimes be difficult for teachers of toddlers to interpret their drawings, but taking notes and making field sketches are usually valuable activities for toddlers, since some can already begin to connect what they see with what they want to represent graphically. A few toddlers and many preschoolers, who are more mature, can make field sketches, paintings, diagrams, and maps to represent what they see. Their representations can reflect things they saw and experienced with some accuracy. One class of four-year-olds went on a field visit to take a close look at watches. Several drew sketches that portrayed the parts of a watch, and some even attempted to label their drawings, including some words they had learned from the experts.

In order to collect memories of the visit, teachers of toddlers and preschoolers can be especially attentive in identifying things they were drawn to. Notes, videos, and photographs taken by the teacher and other accompanying adults can be very valuable for analyzing and reflecting about the experiences that took place.

Figure 8.7   Taking field notes of a clock that attracted his attention

Source: Courtesy of teachers of Eton School in Mexico City.

After the Visit

Upon returning from the field visit, or the following day, teachers can lead a discussion that will help children revisit the experience. They might show photographs to help them remember what they saw and invite the youngsters to arrange them in a sequence following the events that took place. For example, in one class of five-year-olds, a couple of children took a few of the photos, which the teacher had previously selected, and arranged them as follows: "First we got on the bus; then we got to the construction site; next we talked to the experts and saw their tools; after that, we got our clipboards and drew; and then we went back on the bus to return to school." Some toddlers are also able to arrange photographs of the visit in a sequence, especially when the teacher selects just very few of them.

If the children collected samples at the field site, they may want to compare their collection with those of their peers to look at them using a magnifier or organize them by different attributes.

The teacher can also encourage youngsters to share their field sketches with peers and talk about what they drew. This may be helpful for them, as they could be reminded of things that had caught their attention. Furthermore, it could also help teachers identify the children's interests and to group them for subsequent work sessions.

Together as a class, preschoolers could revisit their questions and decide which were answered during the visit and which remained unanswered. The teacher could assess the children's understanding and evaluate whether the youngsters may need further exploration to answer the questions that were addressed during the visit, or whether she could plan opportunities to answer other ones.

In some countries or schools, it may be challenging for teachers to take their class to a field site. This could be due to the age of the children or other safety reasons, traffic problems, lack of funding or transportation, or school policies, among others. There are, however, other or/and additional ways for children to get firsthand information that can enrich a project.

Inviting Experts to Visit the Class and Respond to Questions

Teachers can invite to the classroom an expert who is able to contribute valuable information that enriches understanding of the project topic. An expert could be a parent or a local person skilled in the specific topic. It is usually a good idea for teachers to talk to the experts before their visit and ask them to bring in some material, tools, or equipment. It can also be helpful to inform them about the children's questions to determine which ones they could answer. At times, adults may have little experience talking about objects or about their jobs with young children, and thus, they might include complex technical language that youngsters might not yet be able to understand. On the other hand, some visitors might feel that talking to young children implies amusing them or bringing in treats to make them feel "happy" and motivated. Teachers can explain that young learners do not need amusement items but that they are quite interested in finding out about real things in their world, and that the presence of visitors in their class will be valued because of the information they share.

Figure 8.8   The gardener came to a class of 4-year-olds to teach them how to pot a plant

Source: Courtesy of teachers of Eton School in Mexico City.

Teachers of toddlers must be careful when choosing an expert and take into consideration that the presence of a parent might inhibit their children's usual manner of exploration in the classroom. Subsequently, the children's experience in this situation may not be as fruitful and could also affect the exploration of their classmates.

When experts visit classrooms, children can undertake several activities that are similar to those they would conduct at a field site. They could ask questions, take a close look at objects that were brought into class, watch and participate in different processes, and make field sketches of things that caught their interest. Consider these two examples:

A class of two-year-olds who were doing a project on fruits invited one of the mothers as an expert to show them how to use fruit to make fruit salad. The expert brought in different types of fruits, which the children were able to handle and ask questions about. Then they helped the expert to peel and cut the fruit. Next they experimented with mixing orange juice in with the pieces of fruit, and after that, they all enjoyed eating what they had prepared. Later, the children made sketches of something they remembered from the expert's visit.

During a study of eyes, a class of five-year-olds invited a blind person to answer the following questions:

- How do you know where to go if you can't see?
- How can you write or read?
- How do you pour water into a glass without spilling it?
- How do you paint your nails?

The woman brought her walking cane and showed the children how she moved around. She also brought the tools needed to write in the Braille system and demonstrated how to do it. However, she mentioned that she now rarely used those tools for writing, since computers were friendlier and easier to handle. She took out her computer and showed the children how she used it. The woman also brought books that the children saw and touched after she read a story. She also poured water into a glass and explained that she knew when the glass was getting full by listening to the sound of the water. She also added that it was hard for her to paint her nails on her own, but that her mother helped her do this. The children were able to touch all the tools that were brought to class. They also made field sketches of the different things the expert showed them (writing tools, books, the computer, and the cane), which they talked about during a later discussion with their teacher and peers.

Although some young children may gain some information by looking at books, watching videos, or by viewing images drawn from the Internet, their understanding of the world is most likely best achieved through sensory exploration and firsthand experiences.

HOW CAN YOUNG CHILDREN REPRESENT THEIR UNDERSTANDINGS?

As the study of a topic progresses and the children begin to find answers to some of their questions, they set out to represent what they have learned. The class could be divided into several smaller groups of children who share similar interests in particular sub-topics. For instance, in a study of birds, a group of children might be curious about different species of birds, while another group might be interested in bird anatomy. In this phase of the project, children can work collaboratively or independently to represent their new knowledge and understanding.

How Toddlers and Preschoolers Collaborate and Work Together during the Process of Representation

As previously discussed in chapter 1, collaborative work builds a sense of community in the classroom and offers opportunities for children and adults to learn together and from each other. Project work has a story quality to it that promotes cooperative work. Children go through a sequence of events that involve interactions and collaborative efforts. Even though older children are usually more experienced when working together, young children may also benefit from cooperating with each other to reach a common goal, as it promotes the development of their growing social and emotional competencies. This kind of work encourages youngsters to:

- Notice other children and what they are doing,
- show enthusiasm about the company of their peers, listen to each other,
- begin to understand the intentions of others,
- share materials and tools, take turns, make choices,
- negotiate with others to solve a problem, and
- report their findings to others, and so on.

Toddlers are still at a very egocentric stage of emotional development, and although some might begin to notice and show interest in what their peers are doing, others may not. When encouraged to create something together, they usually work in parallel. They might be physically side by side, or in front of each other but working in their own space and at their own activity.

In one class of two-year-olds, the teacher invited the youngsters to paint a mural of a garden. She set it up in such a way that they needed to share the paintbrushes and different colors of paint. The children chose a space to work on and became engaged in the activity. Some were silent; others started talking to each other about family happenings, places they had been to, or toys they had at home. A few of them talked about the colors they were using to paint or about objects they were depicting: "This is blue," "Mine is orange," "I made a flower," and "My flower is yellow." Some only used one color of paint, while others waited until they saw a paintbrush and paint that was not being used and then proceeded to change colors. Some asked their peers for the color they wanted to use. A few were successful, as their peers willingly shared, while others had some conflicts over the situation. The mural of the garden was made up of individual pieces of work that shared a common space, rather than being a product that reflected collaborative work.

Collaborative work looks quite different as children grow older and more mature. Preschool children are usually interested in participating collectively in experiences. Some of them enjoy working together and take increasing interest in what their peers say and do. They can work cooperatively to reach a common goal in which several skills and steps can be involved. These may include:

- Planning how to carry out the work to be done,
- thinking of the materials that would be needed,
- deciding what each member of the group would do, and
- facing and solving the challenges they encounter as they progress in their work together.

A group of five-year-olds set out to construct a three-dimensional model of an elevator. Together, they attempted to write a list of the materials they would need:

- *Crbd* (cardboard)
- *Scsrs* (scissors)
- *Glu* (glue)
- *Tnfol* (tin foil)
- *Bns* (buttons)
- *Peipr* (paper)
- *Mrcrs* (markers)

Figure 8.9   Children consulting with the teacher to solve problems they faced as they constructed a model of an elevator

Source: Courtesy of teachers of Eton School in Mexico City.

Once they got the supplies, they proceeded to determine who would do what. Two of them would cut the cardboard and put the pieces together in the shape of a box, one would cut the tin foil that would later be wrapped around the cardboard, and the others would draw the buttons and write the numbers and signs that are found inside an elevator. As soon as their work progressed, they faced several challenges: the cardboard was very hard to cut using scissors; the tin foil curled up as they tried to cut it, and as a result, the edges were not very straight; and they couldn't remember the signs or numbers inside an elevator accurately. They began to discuss their problems and started helping each other to solve them. They also consulted with other peers and, at times, asked the teacher for guidance. After several sessions, the children finished their elevator and felt very proud of what they achieved by working together.

Teachers can promote collaborative work by planning experiences where children can work together rather than individually. Youngsters may need significant guidance in learning to interact with others and in working toward achieving a common goal. Although some challenging incidents might occur between them, conflict resolution is a valuable life-long skill that children could begin to practice from the time they are toddlers.

The Exploration of Tools and Materials

Toddlers require ample time to simply explore tools and materials, such as clay, paint, paintbrushes, markers, glue, and scissors, among others. It is helpful if they can do this before learning representational strategies. They often interact with these objects using all of their senses, and it is not uncommon to see them tasting materials or introducing objects into their noses or ears. Teachers should carefully consider the items children will be using and work with small groups to closely supervise sessions of exploration.

Teachers might also need to take the necessary precautions when selecting suitable spaces for children to work in, since it is natural for them to spill water or paint or to use them on surfaces or objects not intended for that purpose. Some teachers may hesitate to encourage children to use different materials, as they might be concerned about safety or the appearance of their classroom. However, when young children are guided in how to use tools and materials, they are usually able and willing to follow the required procedures. It might be a good idea for teachers to feel confident in using different materials themselves in order to guide children in using them. Some children, however, might not feel comfortable when interacting with certain materials. Teachers can be helpful by being respectful and understanding and offering other alternatives for those who might need them.

Some materials and tools for representation that could be used in early childhood classrooms could include: crayons, chalk, markers, watercolors, tempera paint, different kinds of paper, scissors, paintbrushes, glue, glue sticks, wire, small scale hammers, scraps of wood, and pieces of tile, among other discarded materials found in homes and places of work. Teachers might send home a list of things that could be useful in the classroom. Most parents are willing and enthusiastic about collecting items they could contribute to the project.

Figure 8.10   A toddler's exploration of clay using tools

Source: Courtesy of teachers of Eton School in Mexico City.

Especially for toddlers, repeated interactions with the same materials are beneficial, so they can learn about their different properties and characteristics. For instance, on several occasions, clay can be presented to them either in slabs, in balls, in coils, or sometimes together with tools. Teachers can plan these sessions with small groups of children acting as models in guiding them through the possibilities that the different materials and tools offer. Sessions of exploration should be just that, and although teachers may provide guidance, they should not act as directors of the experience or expect an accurately executed finished product.

Some toddlers and preschoolers who have had the opportunity to explore materials for extended periods of time are usually then interested in trying to make things with them. They will often use them purposefully to create things they are familiar with: "I made a dog," "I painted a house," and "This is me."

Teachers might have a variety of materials displayed in the classroom that youngsters could select from to use in their representations. As children become more knowledgeable about the properties of different elements, they may select, with the guidance of their teacher, the ones they would like to use for different purposes or the ones that could be more suitable for specific kinds of representations.

The Processes of Representation

The process of representation involves many valuable cognitive, motor, and social abilities, which children utilize when working toward making and completing a product. The process of representation can also help children to feel a sense of ownership over their work and the satisfaction of accomplishing a goal. During the process of representation, children are engaged in their work, collaborate with others, apply skills, and solve challenges to reach a goal. In addition to the theoretical reasoning behind representation, teachers may also want to consider some of the following practical aspects that could further assist in making this process both a rewarding and successful experience in their classrooms.

The duration of the processes of representation (e.g., drawing, making models, etc.) may vary greatly. It might last for only a session (during a mini-project), or it might take place over the course of several weeks. The time devoted to each working session can also vary. At times, youngsters might be very engaged in their work and might want to work consistently for long periods of time, while at other times, they might have to stop working in order to be able to comply with the schedule that was planned for the day. Some children might feel extremely frustrated when they have just started something and are shortly asked to put it away. Considering the fact that it often takes some time for the children to set out the materials needed to get organized with the members of their group and begin working, it might be a good idea for teachers to consider planning for uninterrupted and lengthy periods of time when children are working on their representations.

Some teachers might have limited space for storage or display in their classrooms. So it might be helpful to consider that, during a project, there could be many products in progress and that their size might be an issue in trying to keep their classrooms organized. Teachers could suggest that children make small-scale models or other representations, which could be adequately stored and kept.

If possible, unfinished products could be kept in the place where the children were working, as it is very satisfying for them to see their work in progress and come back to it the following day. This would also provide all the other youngsters in the class the opportunity to see each other's work and to contribute with comments and suggestions.

Some teachers might feel overwhelmed during this process, as many things might be going on at the same time in the classroom that might demand their guidance. It could be a useful option to invite parents to volunteer to come in and help when children are making representations. However, it is important to coach them on how best to help the children. Some parents might be so eager to please the teacher that they could end up directing the experience or even doing the work themselves. Teachers can guide them by giving examples of things they could do and say and by modeling how to interact with small groups of children when they are working. When parents know what they are expected to do and how to do it, most are quite willing to follow the instructions and learn different strategies.

Occasionally, teachers have commented that sometimes children want to finish their work rapidly, not really caring about its quality. This might be because some children feel they are successful when they conclude a task in as short a time as possible or because many of them have not had the experience of being encouraged to take their time to work on things. Often, children are rushed or asked to comply within limited time frames. Teachers who are experienced in doing project work have learned to slow down and to encourage children to revisit their representations. They guide them in considering other aspects of their work, finishing something that might not be concluded, fixing things that might not be working, or adding more details so that peers and other visitors can more easily understand what they want to communicate.

The Products of Representation

Young children can show their new knowledge by making things or/and representing their experiences. The products of these activities might reflect language and mathematical skills and demonstrate understanding of some scientific and social studies concepts. For example, after collecting leaves that had fallen off some trees in the school's garden, a group of toddlers proceeded to closely examine them. Next, they sorted the leaves into two categories: the big ones and the little ones. As the teacher saw them spontaneously doing this, she suggested that they might want to paste the leaves on a piece of construction paper to make a poster that would show other viewers all the large and small leaves they had found. This same experience looked quite different in a class of preschool children who, after analyzing their collection of leaves, sorted them into the following categories: oval ones, pointy ones, and round ones. With the guidance of their teacher, they made a graph that showed leaves that shared the same attributes and the number they had collected of each. Another group of children in this class separated the green leaves from the brown ones and concluded that the brown ones were dead. They discussed how the different colored leaves were similar and different from each other. The teacher then explained that, by using a Venn diagram, they could represent things that share similarities and differences and taught them how to make one.

Representations might vary considerably in diversity and complexity, depending on the children's level of maturity and ability to use the materials, tools, and representational strategies. Teachers of young children might need to teach them different ways things can be represented. They might teach a group or, more likely, just the one or two toddlers who are interested and ready to learn. As they grow older, children can become more independent in selecting the kinds of products that would best represent their learning. Some forms of representation might be adequate for young children, while others might be best left for use when children are older.

Although there are a wide variety of possibilities through which young children can express their understanding, it could be a good idea for toddlers to start with some of the following:

a) Dramatic play.
   Dramatic play could be carried out with props and items included in the classroom and which children could use to represent experiences, roles different people play, and processes they are learning about.

Figure 8.11   "This is a very tall building."

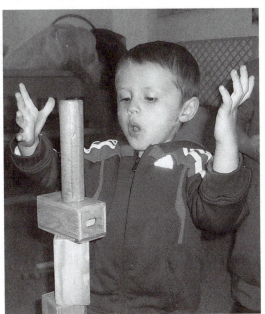

Source: Courtesy of teachers of Eton School in Mexico City.

b) Making models.

Children can make models using clay or other materials to portray objects that are familiar to them. Some teachers have seen that toddlers are better able to express their understandings by making three-dimensional representations than by making two-dimensional ones.

c) Constructions.

Constructions can be made using blocks and other materials, which children may use to represent places and objects, such as buildings, houses, and other familiar locations. Most youngsters take very naturally to block building and usually need little guidance in using them to build things. Children often want to add on to their constructions during the course of several days, so it might be a good idea to leave them in the sites where the youngsters are working.

d) Drawings and paintings.

Figure 8.12   A timeline made by a group of 4-year-olds that shows how plants are watered

Source: Courtesy of teachers of Eton School in Mexico City.

Children may draw or paint scenes, stories, objects, and people. Often these representations might be difficult for adults to understand. Nonetheless, many toddlers are able to comment on their pieces of work and explain what they did. Their scribbles might represent different things, including the sound of an object and/or its movement.

For example, upon returning from taking a close look at a car, a teacher in a classroom of three-year-olds invited them to draw what they had seen and decided to observe one of them while he was drawing. The child took a marker and started drawing many concentric circles on the paper, while making the following sounds: "Rrrum, rrum, rrum." The teacher approached him and asked about his drawing. The child said: "These are the tires going round and round."

Figure 8.13   Children making a map to represent their walk around the block

Source: Courtesy of teachers of Eton School in Mexico City.

When providing sessions for observational drawing, teachers may encourage children to touch, smell, or hear the sound of the object before they attempt to draw it. This could help them to better understand the connection between the object and what they set out to draw.

Some of the more mature toddlers, and many preschoolers, might be able to engage in additional forms of representation that could include making maps, diagrams, charts, graphs, dichotomies, and timelines, among other graphic organizers.

Consider the following examples:

In a class of four-year-olds, children went for a walk around the block. The next day, the teacher printed and displayed some of the pictures of things they had seen. A group of youngsters decided to make a map, which included the school, streets, lampposts, mailboxes, houses, numbers, and signs. As days went by, other children participated in adding details to the representation.

A class of five-year-olds went on a tour on a double decker bus to see different landmarks in the city. The bus made several stops, and the children got off the bus and back on it again several times. Some noticed and commented among themselves that if you don't get back on the bus on time, you might be left behind. Back in the classroom, this group of children shared what they had talked about amongst themselves with the rest of the class. The teacher encouraged them to explore this further and read a brochure that was given to her while on the bus, which contained information about the bus stops and the timetable to be followed. The children concluded that buses needed to comply with a schedule so that people could know when to expect their arrival. They then made a timeline to represent the schedule and the different stops the double decker bus had made during their trip.

Some teachers might at times worry when looking at the representations made by young children, since these might not usually reflect much accuracy. In one school, teachers who first started doing project work felt anxious that parents would be critical of their work, since all the drawings that were to be sent home had very similar scribbles on them, and most parents would probably not be able to understand what their children represented. As these teachers gained more experience in doing project work, they learned to communicate better with others about the work of the children. They now usually add accompanying photographs and narratives when sharing a piece of work. In this way, parents and other visitors are better able to appreciate and understand the children's work. These teachers have also comprehended that the products of representation do not need to be "beautiful" but that their beauty and value lie in the process behind them and the understanding they reflect.

PHASE III: HOW YOUNG CHILDREN CAN SHARE THEIR WORK

As the project comes to a close in the third phase of a project, teachers can revisit the documentation. A detailed description of the process of documentation is addressed in chapter 10. Together, the teacher and children can reflect on the questions that were answered, the processes they followed, the things they made, and those they remember and learned. Teachers can assess individual and collective learning by looking at photographs, reading narratives of events and conversations that took place, and evaluating the products of representation.

In this culminating phase of the project, the collective learning of the group becomes a story to be shared with the members of the community. Young children are as eager and enthusiastic as older learners to share their work with parents, teachers, and peers. They demonstrate ownership and pride when they show pictures of themselves involved in exploration or products of their work to others. Most toddlers are able to point to their work and say: "This is mine," or "I made this" as they show their representations to their parents, other adults, or peers. While looking at the display of the documentation of the project, some more mature toddlers and many preschool children are able to explain processes they went through, places they visited, products they made, and other things they learned.

Some young children are not very talkative at home about what happens at school, while others might share portions of the story of a project that some parents might have difficulty understanding. When parents are given the opportunity to see the conclusion of a project, they become more knowledgeable about this kind of work and are usually better able to understand the value of the processes involved in doing a project. Furthermore, most parents feel much pride when seeing what their children have created and learned and are grateful for having the opportunity to participate in their school life.

Teachers of young children usually decide how the project will be concluded and shared. At times, however, some preschoolers who show more initiative might contribute with ideas for a culminating activity.

For instance: in a class of five-year-olds who were concluding a project on butterflies, a group of children suggested to the teacher that they would like to dress up as different kinds of butterflies. The children in this class, with the guidance of their teacher, made costumes and held a butterfly parade for parents and peers.

There are a wide variety of options that teachers might want to consider to conclude a project. Some might choose to invite visitors to see a display of the documentation of the project. Such a display

Figure 8.14   A teacher sharing the work that took place during the three phases of a project, using a PowerPoint presentation

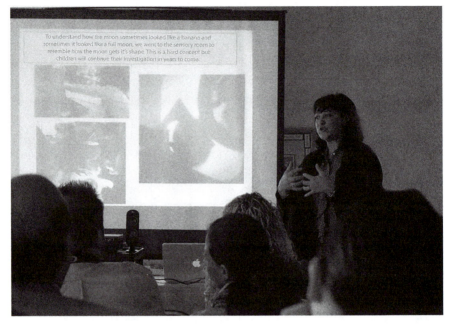

Source: Courtesy of teachers of Eton School in Mexico City.

could include photographs of children at work, narratives or stories to explain the progression of the project, and pieces of work made by the children. Some teachers might want to put together a PowerPoint presentation to show how the project progressed, while others might want to share videos of some of the different events and processes that took place. Many teachers choose to keep a collection of work to make a class book, or place each child's work in a folder that they could take home to share with their parents.

Other teachers might prefer to plan a culminating event where they can show illustrations of the experiences the children had and the knowledge they gained about a topic. Consider the following examples:

To conclude a project on fruits, one teacher of a group of toddlers invited parents to her classroom. She recreated several of the experiences children had during the project and set out objects on different tables for parents and the children to explore together. Most of the toddlers in this class remembered their previous experiences and eagerly took their parents to the different centers in which the activities were offered. On one of the tables, the teacher displayed a wide variety of fruits, which children and parents were invited to sample. Several children pointed at some of the fruits and commented. "Try the mango, Mom, it's good!" said one of them; "I don't like the red one," said another one. On a second table, the teacher placed a cantaloupe, a pineapple, a watermelon, a couple of apples, and a peach. The children and the adults touched them and compared the different textures of their skins. On a third table, the teacher placed fruits that looked different on the outside from the way they looked on the inside. The youngsters and their parents talked about the things they noticed. On a fourth table, children and parents were able to experience how some fruits can be transformed into a liquid, and together, they made orange juice and lemonade.

To culminate their project on bees, a teacher and her class of four-year-olds invited parents and peers to the presentation of their project. The children, who had worked in each of the different interest groups, set up centers where people could get information. They used their representations to teach others information about bees. In one center, visitors could learn about the anatomy of a bee; in a second center, they could learn about different kinds of bees; in a third center, children explained what you can do when you get stung by a bee; and in a fourth center, children showed different bee products used and made by man. Most of these preschool children were quite eloquent, and visitors were impressed with how much they had learned about this topic.

When teachers and children conclude a project, they can revisit their experiences together, reflect on their new knowledge, and feel a sense of pride and joy when sharing their accomplishments with others.

SUMMARY

Project work encourages young children to think deeply and learn a great deal about objects, places, and people they are familiar with. It helps them develop and strengthen their inborn dispositions to find out about things around them as they become more competent in formulating questions, hypothesizing, and coming to conclusions in the process of learning how things work in their world. During the course of a project, toddlers and preschoolers have many opportunities to apply their growing cognitive, social, and emotional skills and to understand how useful these are in their daily lives. Teachers of young children can consider several aspects that could be helpful in making their project experiences successful. These include the selection of the topic, the alternatives for different kinds of investigation, the processes which children go through when representing their understandings, and the different ways their learning can be shared with members of their community.

In the following chapter, you will find many similarities as to how this work is undertaken with older children, and yet you will also find significant differences in the variety of topics that might be addressed, the manner in which research can be conducted, and the different forms of representations that children in the elementary grades can use to represent their understanding.

NINE

Projects in the Elementary School Years

INTRODUCTION

In this chapter, we refer to a few examples of elementary projects teachers have shared with us. One of these is a small-scale project on how the children came to school (Grade 1). Three additional projects are referred to in relation to each phase of the work: a project on the local theater (Grade 2); a project on the city of Durham, N.C. (Grade 3); and a project on corn (Grade 5). Reference is also made to other projects as appropriate to illustrate particular additional points about conducting projects with elementary grade children.

In the elementary school, children's progress is usually based on formal assessment processes. There are elementary grade level standards in each of the curriculum content areas and standards for academic skills that children are expected to master. Throughout the elementary years, student work gradually becomes more formal and is increasingly directed by teachers. In spite of the prevalence of formal standards of achievement, students continue to work to a higher standard when they are interested in what they are doing and see it as meaningful to them and relevant to their own lives. They also usually become more engaged in tasks when they have some influence over the development of the work for at least part of the time (Tomlinson, 2008).

THE BENEFITS OF PROJECT WORK FOR ELEMENTARY STUDENTS

Student interest and intrinsic motivation have long been positively associated with project work. Project topics are chosen for their relevance to students' daily lives and the opportunities they provide for students to conduct firsthand research at field sites near the school. The project approach to teaching and learning in the elementary grades offers teachers a framework of strategies and techniques to enable students to develop alternative ways to do research and to represent their findings. In the early elementary years, the students frequently study topics that allow for firsthand investigation in the neighborhood of the school, such as the nearby park, the supermarket, a local farm or factory, and many other directly observable local phenomena worth understanding in greater depth.

As students grow older, teachers guide them in the study of topics that are further removed from their everyday lives but still relevant in the sense that they are about events, places, objects, materials, and people with a connection to daily life needs, such as water purification, recycling, or the adult world of work.

Usually students in a class study the same broad topic. However, they investigate many different aspects of it through a variety of related subtopics, which can enable individuals or small groups of students with particular interests or skills to make diverse contributions to the work in progress. Students might also be interested in different forms of representation, such as graphs, maps, timelines, charts, Venn diagrams, etc., which they can have some choice in developing either individually or in collaboration with classmates in a small group in order to share the findings of their research.

As students engage in project work, there are many ways for them to appreciate the value and usefulness of language and math skills in the workplace and the community. They learn to take a scientific approach to the investigation of natural phenomena and human interventions in the natural environment. They also develop a geographical and historical sense in relation to the topics as they consider how much comes to them from overseas and what has changed over time to make their current way of life possible.

SELECTING A TOPIC OF STUDY FOR A PROJECT IN THE ELEMENTARY YEARS

Teachers report to us that the topics most successful for a project are those the children see as relevant to them in their everyday lives. The selection of such topics ensures that the students will have some prior experience and knowledge that can form the basis for further study. Real world topics are most likely to have opportunities to visit field sites and invite local experts who can be helpful to the students for first hand experiences and data collection for their study.

Selecting topics that relate to the real world enables students to talk to family members about their own experiences and their understandings and/or expertise related to the topic. The students not only learn within the classroom but can see the significance of the information in the wider world beyond the school. As children grow through the elementary school years, their interests naturally shift from a family-based general knowledge to one that is more local-community based. At the same time, with increasing age they become better able to learn about things which are more remote in historical time or geographical location than their own time, neighborhood, or region.

Projects on various aspects of the environment in the early elementary years can focus on nearby phenomena such as a local river, mountain, forest, lake, or ocean shoreline. As students gain more experience of their immediate surroundings and learn more formal and abstract knowledge in the upper elementary grades, their interest can easily shift to understandings about distant rivers, mountains, oceans, etc., in the world. In the same way, a project which is carried out in the early grades on how decisions are made by different groups of people in a family, a school, or a local community can provide basic knowledge that underpins a project in the upper elementary years on business management, or local, state, or federal government. Teachers can in this way appreciate how local and small-scale topics that are ideal for study through a project in the early years in school provide basic understandings to support learning in the more abstract or distant upper elementary curriculum in the subject areas of science, social studies, and health.

WHAT IS THE TYPICAL DURATION OF A PROJECT IN THE ELEMENTARY CLASSROOM?

Most projects last from 6 to 8 weeks. This gives the teacher and students time to delve in depth into the various subtopics in which students can typically become interested. Time is needed for the teachers to support the growing interest of students, to elicit their research questions, to provide field experiences, and to offer appropriately selected secondary sources of information to increase their knowledge. Teachers need time to develop the project with the students through providing resources for representational work and developing ways for the students to share with others what they have found out about the topic and what they have learned from their investigation.

However, while the longer-term projects are usually timed for the fall and the spring, there might be several other times in the school year for small scale mini-projects to be valuable for student learning. Here is an example of a mini-project carried out at the beginning of the year when the teacher is getting to know the students and establishing routines for social interaction and the use of resources in the classroom.

Example of a Mini-Project: How We Come to School

In one classroom, a group of first graders talked about how they came to school. This provided the starting point for a mini-project in which the teacher was able to assess the students on various skills and strategies needed for project study: discussion, field experience, representation, investigation, collaboration, and sharing of information through displays of work in the classroom. At the same time, the students were able to apply academic skills at various levels of difficulty in the course of the work.

Discussion

The project work began with the students telling personal stories about coming to school and what happened along the way. The students were able to share how they came, whether on foot, by car, or on the school bus. They also talked about whether their parents or older siblings accompanied them or whether they came alone. They talked about how far they came, how long it took them, and what happened if they were late. They talked about the period of getting ready to leave for school in the morning. They talked about what they usually saw on the way to school and how the weather affected them. The teacher wrote the most relevant vocabulary on chart paper as the students used the words in their stories and discussion. She grouped the words as she wrote them so that the words applying to the same subtopic were seen in the same area on the chart paper. For instance, words about vehicles were grouped together (car, bus, bicycle, etc.), as were words relating to how you give directions to someone so they can find their way easily (left, right, up, down, after, etc.), and so on.

Some students were quite comfortable sharing their experiences through oral storytelling, while others were more willing to do so when they had drawings or paintings to refer to as they talked. The teacher asked questions to invite students to give more details or helped other students to ask questions they might have about the experiences that were being shared. Some students identified with others, and some had different or even unique means of transportation. Some came from outside the town, through the center of town, or over the river, while other students came from the immediate neighborhood of the school. As disagreements arose when they remembered conflicting information about their experiences, the teacher helped the students express these as questions to be investigated later. One disagreement among the children concerned whether you could see the town hall clock from the bridge over the river or not. This provided the opportunity for the teacher to develop the following question with the students: "Can you see the town hall clock from the bridge over the river?" This was a fact that could easily be checked during a field visit. Some questions were a little more challenging to investigate.

Field Experience

The knowledge content for this project lay mostly with the students since it was a project on a topic which was entirely within their own experience. However, while each child had intimate knowledge of his or her own way to school, they had little knowledge about the experiences of their classmates. The research was therefore mostly about the collective experience of this class of students coming to school each day.

The field work was unusual in this mini-project in that it was limited to exploring differences of opinion or sharing the firsthand experiences of a few students so that the whole class could learn about "How we come to school." One day, the students engaged in this project walked with one of the girls in the class and her father to and from her home not far from the school. The children learned about safety rules for walking on the sidewalks, across driveways, and the side roads. They timed the walk to school and measured the distances in numbers of steps from one part of the walk to the next. They made notes on clipboards of what they learned and saw along the way. They noted the street lamps, stop signs, mailboxes, garbage bins, enclosures (walls, fences, hedges, etc.), notices (Beware of the Dog, house names), parked vehicles, commercial vehicles, etc.

They also followed up questions to which they had predicted answers, such as: If you cross the bridge over the river, do you come to the town center next? Is there a post box on the crossing two blocks from the school? Do all the houses have mailboxes? Can you see the town hall clock from the bridge over the river? and so on.

Representation

The students told their personal stories at group time. They also made drawings and paintings from memory to illustrate their stories. They wrote captions to the drawings and labeled them. For example, one child drew a picture of traffic lights and wrote the caption, "My dad has to stop when the lights are red," and another drew a picture of a bridge with the caption, "I can see the river. There are ducks."

Two students collected data for a bar chart to represent the different ways students came to school, and the teacher helped them to draw up the chart showing the numbers of students in each category. Other students made a map of the school neighborhood after one of the field experiences. Another group of students represented the distances between various landmarks in the town. Some students were interested to represent the amounts of time different classmates had to spend coming to school. They researched the times each student left home each day to come to school. Some students were surprised to learn that others went first to day care for a time on the way to school. Some students who experienced day care were surprised to find that other students came to school straight from home.

Investigation

The research undertaken in the course of this project took place mostly in the classroom, with students learning from one another's experiences or in the neighborhood of the school. There was little need for secondary source research using books, videos, or the Internet, although maps were a great help for the more advanced students in this class. Students interviewed each other. They talked about how they came to school by different means and compared their experiences. They represented the information in a Venn diagram.

It was easy to involve family members in helping with the project, as the knowledge they had to share was readily accessible. Parents talked about the value of walking to school compared with going by car, and others explained the positive value of going to school by car. Different points of view were discussed and appreciated.

The school bus driver was able to come to the classroom and served as a visiting expert. The children asked her about driving and maintaining the bus and about the challenges of driving in the morning traffic compared with the relatively empty roads in the afternoon.

Display

The teacher had several pieces of children's work to display in the classroom and in the hallway throughout the two weeks. First were the drawings and paintings of coming to school, with word labels and captions, and the written stories students had to share. In the second phase of the project, various questions were investigated, and written reports, charts, maps, timelines, Venn diagrams, etc., were posted to enable students to learn about the experiences their classmates had coming to school. The sharing also showed students how much it was possible to learn about the topic of how students come to school. They did indeed develop a rich understanding of the topic from several different points of view: those of the students themselves, their parents, day care providers, the drivers of vehicles, the teacher, and so on.

One of the main purposes of displaying documentation in the classroom is to show the many ways it is possible for students to investigate questions and represent their findings. Students become familiar with these as they use them in successive projects. In the third phase of a project, it can be very helpful to conclude the work with a culminating event to which parents can be invited to see what their children have been learning. In the case of a mini-project, this might or might not be a useful occasion. The study might be concluded in two or three weeks from the start of the term before launching a more major project.

The Benefits of a Mini-Project

The project described here showed how these students could become very involved in their learning when it was a topic that interested them. In a sense, they were the ones who possessed much of the information being sought by their classmates. It is also easy to see how this topic might be appropriate for first grade children but not of sufficiently challenging scope for third graders. In third grade, it would be more appropriate to choose a topic that would involve the students in carrying out some secondary source research in books or through the Internet.

Teachers find such mini-projects useful early in the school year because the students are not all doing the same work. They are selecting much of the work they do based on their interests and their academic strengths. As they are writing, counting, measuring, collecting data, etc., they are applying academic skills independently that they have been taught the previous year and that the teacher might be reviewing alongside the project in the more teacher-directed aspects of the program.

In the mini-project described here, one of the goals for the teacher was to find out how well the students could engage in project work at the beginning of the school year. How well could they do the following?

- tell personal stories
- express their curiosity
- discuss different points of view in a group
- ask questions
- use different forms of representation
- use firsthand experience in the field to answer questions
- integrate new information with past knowledge
- work together with classmates
- share ongoing work and completed representations with others

The mini-project on "How we come to school" allowed for assessment of students' varying abilities. Some students are at much more advanced levels in some of the above areas than others. In their academic work, some students are reluctant or unable to use some writing or math skills. In the area of social skills, the teacher can quickly learn which students are able to work easily alongside others and which are more successful working alone. A mini-project early in the school year can be helpful in identifying the kind of additional help some students might need and which students should be supported in undertaking more advanced work than would normally be expected of them at their grade level. A mini-project can also be useful during the school year when there is insufficient time to develop an extended project. Sometimes between longer projects or toward the end of a term, it might be appropriate to include a mini-project in the program while recognizing its inherent limitations in terms of time for extended research. One school used a school-wide mini-project on topics associated with the upcoming winter break as the basis for an event that parents were invited to share at the close of the term in December: individual classes worked on the topics of bells, lights, snow, winter sports, celebrations, and family traditions. School-wide mini-projects can allow for school staff discussions about the implementation of the project approach throughout their school.

Projects That May Last for Six to Eight Weeks or Longer

We have looked in detail at the development of a mini-project. We will now explore the advantages of a full-scale project with reference to several projects shared with us by teachers in elementary classrooms. The examples provided will show how teachers plan and develop projects, bearing in mind the elementary curriculum for their grade level.

A full-scale project allows the investigative work to extend over a longer period of time, usually from six to eight weeks but sometimes even longer. There can also be time and opportunity to make several field visits and to include a variety of guest experts to come to the classroom during the course of the project. Students have time to familiarize themselves with the main aspects of the project, to learn about the research other students are doing, and to understand their own work in the context of the wider project topic. The longer time frame also allows the teacher to take time in mini-lessons or small group-directed work to make sure that the curriculum benchmarks and standards are addressed as the project progresses. At the end of a full-scale project, it is possible to see major benefits in the students' learning as measurable by more formal testing of curriculum material covered in the project.

TEACHER PLANNING FOR A PROJECT

Compared with other approaches to teaching and learning in the elementary years, projects involve the teacher in less preparation in terms of specific objectives to be covered by students from day to day. However, there is important preparation and planning of a different kind to be done before getting started on a project. Project work involves the teacher in on-going decision-making in the course of the work with students in the classroom. This decision-making is facilitated by the teacher's anticipation of the

Figure 9.1   Teacher's web of the topic of the weather

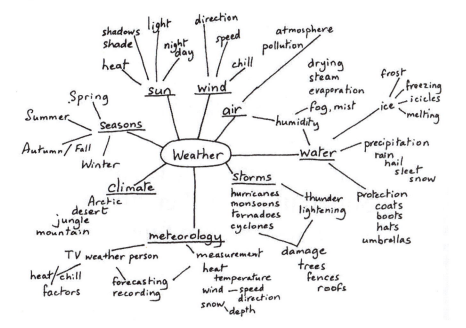

possible alternatives that might present themselves during the sessions.

First of all, teachers can benefit from thinking through the topic in detail and anticipating its value for student learning. We recommend that teachers explore the topic thoroughly at first through preparing a topic web. The term "topic web" is used to refer to a kind of "concept map" or diagram that suggests relationships between words that are related to the same topic in various ways. It is a graphic tool used to organize and structure knowledge. In the way teachers use it, a topic web is a diagram with the topic or main idea at the center and branching out into a number of subtopics. Relevant words are listed under each subtopic or different aspect of the main topic. Through developing such a diagram, the teacher can explore a number of potential avenues of investigation related to the topic. The vocabulary categorized within each subtopic serves to anticipate these possible lines of inquiry with some precision.

Following the development of the topic web, it is possible to generate a list that could be in web format or simply a listed collection of skills and knowledge associated with different areas of the curriculum that would be best applied in the service of these various potential lines of inquiry. Here is a list that was completed by a teacher who was planning to develop a project on weather with a class of third grade students:

3rd Grade Weather Project

Standards and Content

Science as Inquiry

Through active exploration of their environment, students will work individually and in collaboration to:

- Ask questions about objects and organisms
- Formulate hypotheses
- Plan and conduct investigations, keeping constants and changing variables
- Employ standard equipment and tools to gather data
- Conduct interviews and gather information from secondary sources
- Collect, represent, and analyze data
- Make predictions and analyze change
- Communicate and display findings in varied ways, including charts and graphs

Environmental Science

- Observe and describe weather by measurable quantities: temperature, wind direction, wind speed, and precipitation
- Assess weather changes from day to day and over the seasons
- Determine the three states of matter: solid, liquid, and gas
- Observe changes in state due to heating and cooling in common materials

- Using shadows, observe the movement of the sun in the sky during the day
- Observe the angular position of the sun at noon over several months and relate to seasons
- Observe the change in shape of the moon from day to day over several months to determine a pattern

Math

- Solve problems involving measurement and estimation of intervals of time, liquid volumes, and masses of objects
- Represent and interpret data
- Read thermometers to nearest degree (Fahrenheit and Celsius)
- Design investigations to address a question and consider which data-collection method to use
- Collect data using observations, surveys, and experiments
- Represent data through tally charts, tables, bar graphs, and line plots
- Find maximum, minimum, and range
- Summarize and interpret data

Reading

When reading informational texts, students should be able to:

- Ask and answer questions to demonstrate understanding of the text, referring explicitly to the text for answers
- Determine the main idea of a text and key details that support the main idea
- Determine the meaning of domain-specific words
- Use text features (e.g., table of contents, index, tables) and search tools to locate information relevant to a given topic
- Read and comprehend science and technical texts

Information Literacy

- Begin to learn and use the effective formats for presentations (e.g., oral, print, graphical, video, audio, multimedia)

- Recall information from experiences or gather information from print and digital sources, take brief notes on sources, and sort evidence into provided categories

Writing

Write informative/explanatory texts to examine a topic and convey ideas and information clearly

a. Introduce a topic and group-related information together; include illustrations when useful to aiding comprehension
b. Develop the topic with facts, definitions, and details
c. Use linking words and phrases (e.g., also, another, and, more, but) to connect ideas within categories of information
d. Provide a concluding statement or section
e. Conduct short research projects that build knowledge about a topic

Once the teacher has chosen the topic and assessed its potential contribution to learning, the first phase begins when the teacher embarks on the study with the students in the classroom.

Phase I: How Do You Start a Project?

As described in chapter 2, the first phase of a project is when the teacher introduces the topic in an interesting way and invites the students to tell, draw, or write about experiences they have had that are relevant to their current understanding of the topic. The opening discussion that emerges among students from such storytelling ensures that they refer first to their own experience as a primary source of knowledge about a topic. They are not only reciting what they remember from earlier study, from reading about the topic, or from having been told about it. The students are sharing the understanding they have of the topic based on their personal experience of it.

The students will have no personal experience that seems directly relevant with some topics that are typically studied in the upper elementary grades, like former times in history, the American Civil War, local government, or concerning remote experiences like immigration. However, they could begin discussing their personal understandings in the following ways:

The American Civil War: the students can discuss their understanding of "wars," why they happen, the forms they take, how they are resolved, etc. They can think about the necessary vocabulary for talking about escalating conflict: discussion, disagreement, argument, row, fight, battle, etc. They can share experiences of conflict resolution: giving way, conceding certain positions, reaching agreement, making up, etc. They can discuss their understanding of the contrasting words: "war" and "peace."

Immigration: they might discuss "moving house," with reference to why and how people move from one place to another. They can discuss the topic with their parents and grandparents at home or with others they know who have recently moved to a new location, etc.

Local Government: they might discuss personal experiences of how decisions are made affecting groups of people, what they buy in the supermarket, where they go on holiday, opening and closing times for schools or stores, where a new park might be located in a neighborhood, etc.

The purpose of such early discussion of a topic is for the teacher to assess the background knowledge of the students with a view to building a basis for further study based on their own experience. Such an approach helps students to see the relevance of the topic to their own lives. During the discussion of personal stories, students can be encouraged to think of questions they can investigate through research online, in books, and through inviting experts to the classroom from local museums, services, businesses, or government, and interviewing grandparents and elderly neighbors for their experiences.

The Corn Project

One class of fifth grade students in Mexico City undertook a project on corn. The topic of this project arose as the class was reading a lesson from the required history textbook. The lesson talked about the discovery and use of corn in Pre-Hispanic times. The following day, the teacher brought a few books with pictures of how people used corn and set these out on a table with a basket of different colored corn cobs. The students looked at the books individually and in pairs and came together afterward to discuss the topic of corn with a view to starting a project on the topic.

The next day, the students recorded their personal stories through writing and drawing. Many decided to write their stories using a computer. Most of them told stories that were drawn from their everyday life experiences, since corn is eaten as part of most meals in Mexico. As they talked about their experiences, the teacher encouraged them to think about questions they might seek answers to in their investigation of the topic of corn. She also noted which students knew more and which students had not thought much before about corn. She observed which students were interested in the different subtopics that emerged as they listed relevant vocabulary and prepared to sort the words into categories: corn as food, growing corn, selling corn, transporting corn, products made from corn, jobs associated with the corn industry, corn in times past, and corn in other countries, etc. These groups of words were then used to develop a topic web that students could consult for specialized vocabulary and add to throughout the duration of the project.

During the first phase of a project, teachers can learn about what is most interesting to individual students about the topic and what they would like to find out more about. In matching up students' interests and possible areas of research with requisite curriculum content, the teacher can ensure that the project addresses the knowledge and skills the students are required to learn at their grade level in all the subjects. Before the end of the first phase, which might take a few class sessions, the students in discussion with the teacher can formulate a list of questions to guide the investigation in the second phase of the project. The following list of questions launched the students into the second phase of their project on corn:

Why are there different colors of corn?

Where else aside from Mexico does corn grow?

Is corn only used as food?

Why was corn important in Pre-Hispanic cultures?

Table 9.1   Questions-Predictions-Findings Chart made by students studying corn

Questions	Predictions	Findings	How we found the information
Why are there different colors of corn?	Because they grow from different kinds of maize plants.	Corn kernels have different colors because of their individual genes. Each kernel on the cob is a separate entity with their own genes, yet they form on the same cob; just like brothers and sisters in the same home, each is different, but they live together.	Our Science lab teacher acted as our expert and explained that there are breeds or kinds within a type of plant, just as there are breeds of dogs. She brought different types of kernels, and we classified them according to particular characteristics.
Where else aside from Mexico does corn grow?	In the Middle East and India, because I know they eat flatbreads that look like tortillas.	Flatbreads in the Middle East and India are made out of wheat. But there are many countries that have a higher corn production than Mexico. The United States is the highest ranking corn producing country in the world.	By researching on the Internet, we found a site called www. indexmundi.com where we obtained the information to answer our question.
Is corn only used as food?	Yes, because everybody in Mexico eats tortillas, and it is also fed to livestock.	No, corn is used for many different things, and food is only one of them. Actually, industrial use is even more important in terms of money.	We read the labels of all kinds of products looking for corn-related ingredients. We were surprised to discover that corn is used to make medicines, paint, soft drinks, and many other products in our country and in the world.
Why was corn important in Pre-Hispanic cultures?	It was very important as food, and it was included in ceremonies.	It was important as food, but it was also very important in their religious ceremonies. Pre-Hispanic cultures thought that Man had been made out of corn.	In the History textbook and our visit to the National Museum of Anthropology.

These questions were explored through recording students' predictions of possible answers to their questions. When students make such predictions, they frequently become more curious about finding answers to their questions. Their minds are also more prepared to think about the facts they can learn from an expert, a field site, or from some secondary source of information. The first two columns in the chart are completed before engaging in the research, and the findings are added later as well as the final column about how the students found the information. This process of doing research is learned by means of similar steps at any age or stage of learning. On page 189 is a Questions-Predictions-Findings chart made by the students studying corn.

Phase II: Developing the Project

Conducting Field Work

The Durham Project

In this third grade project on the local city of Durham in North Carolina, some students studied the emergency services, their role, how they worked, and who paid for them. Before a visit to the fire station to learn about how people worked there, the students generated the following list of questions to be investigated:

To find out at the Fire Station:

1. How many rooms are there?
2. How many fire trucks are there?
3. How many fire fighters are there?
4. What were the most fires they had to fight in a day?
5. What time do the fire fighters go to bed?
6. How did fire trucks change over the years?
7. What was the biggest fire they had to put out?
8. When was the fire station built?
9. What happens if a fire truck breaks down?
10. What kind of work is there to do at a fire station?

11. How many people work there?

12. How many men work there?

13. How many women work there?

From this list, it can be seen that the students were interested in the scale of the work that the fire station was responsible for. They wanted to know about number and size of the operations carried out. In addition to the number of people and vehicles involved, the students were interested in the lives of the fire fighters. The question about when fire fighters go to bed could lead third graders to learn about a day in the life of a fire fighter: getting up, meal times, work times, rest times, snack times, family time, and bed time. Discussion of the amount of work in terms of hours could lead them to understand what is involved in the work and the difference between routine schedules, practice runs, training, maintenance of equipment, or night work, as well as the emergency response work that would be involved. The question about when the fire station was built would very likely link with other questions about the history of the town and the buildings in it.

Part of the classroom wall documentation on the fire station included the list of questions with the answers the children had collected. In addition, there was a report that listed three pieces of information the students had gained in addition to the information they had specifically sought:

1. Most of the fire station's expenses are paid for through taxes.

2. The ladder on the ladder truck is 75 feet long. That might not seem a lot, but it is!

3. One of the trucks holds 3,000 gallons of water for the hose so that if there isn't a fire hydrant anywhere nearby, the fire fighters can use that water for the hose.

A great deal of the research for this project was conducted through field work and visits to the classroom by guest experts. The teacher, Jeff, had discovered over the years, however, that teaching students how to conduct primary research is critical. Before their first field experience, Jeff explained, "You are going to learn about this place so that you can explain what you learn to your classmates. To do this, you will need to think and act like a researcher, to gather information that you will share with your classmates." The class charted the important qualities of a researcher and referred to the list before each field experience and guest expert.

1. Listen attentively to our guide and don't talk. You'll see buildings and statues, but you won't know why they are important unless you listen. As you listen, you will learn why this site is relevant to our understanding of the city.
2. You will see artifacts. You won't know why these are important unless you read the placard beside them. When you read information that you find interesting, write it down.
3. You will have many questions. Write them down to ask when it is time to do so.
4. Write down information that seems important, such as the names of people, places, and dates.
5. Use your clipboard and pencil to sketch and take notes or your camera to take pictures that will help us understand the city better.

The students visited the following sites of interest: Downtown Durham, including historic sites (the original train station, the crossroads where the tobacco farmers came to town to sell their crops) and new sites, such as the American Tobacco Complex (once a tobacco factory and now the home of National Public Radio, private offices, and restaurants), Duke University, and the new Performing Arts Center.

They toured historic sites: a tobacco plantation, and the tobacco museum. They visited government sites: the city hall, the library, and the court house.

Guest experts to the classroom included a former librarian, who grew up in racially segregated Durham and experienced firsthand the changes of the Civil Rights movement, and a former mayor, who spoke about the job of mayor and city council members. After each experience, students spent several days discussing and documenting what they had learned.

The Theater Project

One second grade class studied their local theater during an eight-week-long project. The teacher had a background in community theatre and thought about the curriculum standards that could be addressed in such a project.

The students worked on the project in some of their regular lessons as well as during the time specially designated for project work. The children studied folk tales in a scheduled reading lesson in which the focus was on developing students' reading fluency. They took roles in reading dramatic versions of the folk tales. In Social Studies, they studied types of employment in their community that were related to the theater and how producers and consumers are essential to a local economy. The discussion of folk tales from around the world drew the children's attention to the similarities and differences among different cultural traditions. Students developed their mapping skills as they worked to appreciate where the people with these cultures were located in the world.

On field visits, it is useful for students to take detailed field notes that they can refer to later when they are back in the classroom. During their field work, these students visited local theaters and recorded what they saw. They drew sketches, took photographs, and wrote brief notes. Some students made sketches and notes about lighting, some about the sets, and others about the concessions. When they returned to school, they discussed what they had learned and added details and labels to their sketches, photographs, and writing. They posted them on the board for future reference.

This second grade class invited several visitors to their classroom to help with their research. Kathy, the school's curriculum director, shared her collection of Cinderella tales from around the world and spoke about the similarities and differences in the stories. Martin, a third grade teacher, was their Audition Expert. He told the students how people audition for parts and how directors decide who gets what part. Isabel, one student's mother, taught them about marketing. They learned important concepts for naming their company; designing a logo; and making signs and flyers, programs, and tickets. Sarah visited and taught them about the importance of costumes. She showed books and samples from various countries and told them that wearing authentic pieces of clothing helped tell the story. When they decided to perform Lon Po Po as one of their plays, a student from China offered to lend some girls clothes that belonged to his sister. His father taught them how to pronounce some of the words authentically, and they learned that Lon Po Po is pronounced "Lon Pou Pou."

When students can learn firsthand from field visits and visiting experts, the information they gain is more memorable than if they had acquired it only through a secondary source of information like a book or a video presentation. They have the opportunity to ask questions and engage in discussion as they think about what they are learning. Following these visits, classroom discussion can be lively and lead to further exploration of the issues in books and through the Internet, and to presentations using video and other digital media.

Representation

One of the best ways to ensure that new information is accurately remembered and well understood is to enable students to represent their new knowledge in writing, drawing, building models, preparing computer presentations, or engaging in role play. As students grow through the elementary years, they can become very competent at using construction materials of various kinds, drawing and painting, planning, and engaging in role play. Additionally, current technology offers new possibilities for representation. These include digital resources such as Prezi or wikispaces, videogames that develop and foster creativity (such as Minecraft, which enables students to create amazing 3D representations), or applications and software that help students make videos, such as iMovie and trailer making apps. Some of these activities can be done alone, some with a partner or in a small group. The students become used to the practice of sharing their representational work with the purpose of demonstrating what they have learned about the topic. They look at each other's work to learn about the findings their classmates are representing. This is especially important because not all students are interested in the same subtopics or doing the same representational work. Representations provide self-assessment challenges. Students are able to see where their knowledge is insufficiently detailed or clearly stated to provide accurate data for classmates who will study their work for information.

It is helpful for the teacher to encourage students to critique and discuss each other's work in terms of how it helps them all to understand the topic more fully. Students can be perceptive in helping others improve their work during the process of its development. The displays of completed work should provide the narrative of how the whole class group sought and acquired particular information and how they came to understand its significance in relation to the topic.

In the theater project, there were many opportunities for students to engage in purposeful writing: letters, applications, invitations, descriptions, conversations, plans, critiques, and reports, etc. Math skills were essential to planning the performances and marketing them in the location they had available in the school. There were also technical challenges to setting up suitable lighting and sound effects. Students worked together and separately in various capacities to bring the plays to performance standard and to ensure the success of their theatre performance.

The Corn Project

The students went to the Museum of Anthropology in Mexico City in their quest for information about corn and how it featured in the lives and culture of the Mayan people. Here is a page of one student's field notes taken on this visit.

In the corn project, an anthropologist came to class to talk about the importance of corn in Pre-Hispanic times and how it was used by the indigenous people. She explained that in the Mayan culture, there was a God of Corn, and she showed several paintings found in objects such as pottery, murals, and archeological sites. She also talked about ceremonies dedicated to corn, which still take place in some small towns in Mexico. After the expert's visit, a group of children set out to paint a mural, trying to include all of the elements they saw in photographs and heard about from the expert. This included what they were learning that was important about corn in Pre-Hispanic culture.

Before embarking on the process of making the mural, the students reviewed what they had learned from the visiting experts.

Figure 9.2   Field notes taken by a 5th grade student

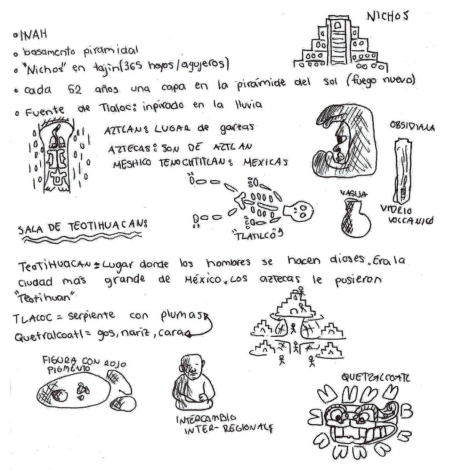

Source: Courtesy of teachers of Eton School in Mexico City.

They conducted research using the Internet and wrote a list of different elements that can be included in murals and they discussed their significance. They decided which they would incorporate in their representation. They made sketches of symbols and ideas included in illustrations that they found through their research. They held discussions as to the story their mural would tell and the elements they needed to include. They continued this process by making a collaborative first draft sketch of what their mural would

Figure 9.3   Grade 5 students' mural depicting symbolic references to corn growth in the Mayan Culture

Source: Courtesy of teachers of Eton School in Mexico City.

look like. Next they set out to paint the mural, making reference to their sketch.

The students then set out to write the story of what they had represented in their mural. As they engaged in discussions to begin this process, they realized they were unsure of some of the specialized vocabulary (such as the name of some gods and the uses of some of the tools that they had represented). They then decided to conduct research on the Internet once again to find the information they needed. The mural took over 8 sessions to complete, as the elements in it were small and included much detail. They wrote several drafts of the story's text. Then they edited their grammatical and spelling errors and proceeded to write it using the computer. After printing it, they made a book, which they placed by their painting so that visitors could read the story the mural told as well as the significance of the different elements included in it.

Investigation

The processes of representation involve students in continuously assessing and adding to their own growing understanding. The processes of representation and investigation are interactive ones. For example, a group of students embarked on a sketch for a model and discovered that some of the dimensions necessary to represent a building were missing from their field notes. They consulted a website and a book for further information in order to proceed with their model. Once they had the basic shape constructed, they decided to provide a platform for the model that would show its location at the edge of a park and close to a city intersection. In order to place the building accurately in its geographical context, the students had to further investigate the precise distances around the structure.

Much investigation is done firsthand at a field site or in discussion with experts, who can be invited to the classroom to share their knowledge and experience with the students. Information provided in this way is frequently more interesting to the students than information from a text book. Students can also follow up initial questions with additional ones when they hear what the experts have to say. Once the students are in the elementary school, however, there are many secondary sources of information they can consult. School librarians and specialists in information technology can be available to teachers in support of the research students undertake in the course of a project.

In some schools, textbooks might no longer be used in traditional class lessons but can be consulted for information that is relevant to the project topic. For the younger children, the teacher can print out material from the Internet with some modification of the vocabulary where necessary. In some classrooms, teachers make a research table available to display sources of information that the students may consult in their project work. Sometimes parents and/or visiting experts can lend books or other printed materials to the students for the duration of the project. These could be placed in the classroom research center. Students can be invited to select materials to take to the place where they are working in a group. They can read and discuss the information relevant to the representations they are currently working on. From time to time, a teacher might work with a group of younger students in a mini-lesson in order to help them read the material provided for them to study. Sometimes such informational reading for the project work can take place at other times in the curriculum. There might be, for example, some flexibility in the program for the teacher to select texts for helping students to read for information in a reading lesson.

Scheduling Project Work Sessions

Many teachers find it useful to schedule a project work session for longer than a regular class lesson period. This allows time for students to develop work individually or in groups with discussion and planning as well as working on particular representations. Frequently these periods of work begin with an orientation with reference to the previous project session. Students are reminded of what can be accomplished on that day and encouraged to organize themselves to continue work that was in progress at the close of the previous project session.

Most of the time would include students working at different tasks alone, in pairs, or in small groups. A visitor to the classroom might see a group of students in discussion about how to proceed with their work. Other students might individually be involved in writing, math calculation, sketching, painting, or other constructional activity. Still others might be sitting around a table in discussion with the teacher about the direction they will be taking in their representational or investigative work for the session.

Typically the students can be working while the teacher is working with a group, talking with an individual student, or moving from one part of the classroom to another. During this time, a teacher can learn a great deal about how the students' understanding of the topic is developing. He can redirect individuals or groups with small-scale interventions, offering a book, suggesting alternatives, listening to discussion, and giving students confidence in the direction they are proposing to take with their work.

The teacher is in the role of a consultant, guide, and mentor. He or she can provide students with a model of how to be effective as a learner and investigator. The teacher does not need to be an expert on the topic but can show students how to explore and to inquire. Students can also learn how to refer to their different sources of information as they represent what they have learned.

The role of the teacher in traditional direct instruction lessons is different. In those contexts, it is important for the teacher to be able to give clear instructions and to support the students in carrying out tasks in pre-specified ways. This can be important for lessons in which all students are being taught new skills in math or language, for example. The tasks have to be correctly done, whereas the project work is more speculative, reflecting ongoing investigation. The same teacher can fulfil these different roles according to the context, and the students can learn the different learning cultures and expectations required of them.

Phase III

Once the teacher has judged that the students have learned a sufficient amount about the topic, she can discuss with them ways they might bring the work to a close. This can be a decision based on a discussion with the whole class. From the teacher's point of view, it is taken with the level of student interest in mind, the amount of information the students have acquired, evaluation of student achievement, the scope of the project, and the time available for further study. Once it is clear that the work should be concluded, it is appropriate to move to the third phase of the project and plan how students will share their new knowledge with other members of their community.

Many teachers conclude a project with some kind of culminating event during which the students share their work with others. This sharing provides an opportunity for students to talk about their work and demonstrate what they have learned with the aid of the representations they have completed. The work of the third phase is mostly fine-tuning, adding explanatory details, self-assessment, facilitating group critiques, and review.

Parents can be invited to see the work at an event at which the members of the class share their project work. As the students become more familiar with project sharing throughout the elementary grades, they can become more active in planning and organizing the closing event. A frequent pattern for the occasion is for the teacher to introduce the students and outline the way the work is to be shared. Then students take over the roles of introducing one another as each student or group of students comes forward to share their knowledge. The rehearsal for such an event does not need to be too extensive, as students have usually become familiar as they talked to their classmates about their work during the course of its development.

The event might take the form of a performance, tour of a museum, participatory simulation, or exploration activities that parents can engage in alongside the students. Sometimes the event might include elements of all of these possibilities.

There are naturally arising opportunities for review in the process of preparing for such a culminating event. This review process can provide the teacher with assessment information for the whole class and for individual students. The assessment can be done in relation to standards across a wide range of curriculum subjects. It can take the form of small tests administered to the whole class. Different groups of students can themselves be involved in selecting questions that would assess what other students might learn from their representations.

Usually the third phase does not take very long, maybe a week or two. It is based on work already completed or nearing completion in the second phase. While some students are completing ongoing work, others are working on the plans or logistics of the sharing event. There are many ways to have all students continue to be active in project-related work right up to the end of the project. In contrast with direct instruction lessons or sequences of lessons in particular disciplines, students have a good deal of opportunity to learn in depth, to develop their understanding of a topic over time, and to feel pride in their personal and group accomplishments. The culminating event allows the students to tell the story of their learning through the documentation of the project that has been progressively accumulated throughout its development.

SUMMARY

In this chapter, we have discussed the project approach with special reference to teaching and learning in the elementary school years. Several examples of projects were examined in detail. The material referred to was drawn from the documentation of projects undertaken by teachers in various schools. Usually in the elementary school, much of the learning is quite formal and takes the form of direct instruction lessons. However, in project work students benefit from being more personally engaged in their learning as it is implemented alongside the more traditional part of the program.

The following chapter addresses the value of drawing in relation to the project approach. Drawing is a representational strategy that is basic to much student work both in the early years and later throughout the elementary school years.

TEN

Documentation and the Project Approach

The term "documentation" is increasingly used to describe various ways of exhibiting and recording important aspects of learning throughout the preschool and primary years of education. The formal dictionary definition of the term "documentation" refers to materials that provide official or visible information or evidence that serves as a reliable record of activities of interest. Sometimes "documentation" is defined as official evidence that serves as a record of events that can be examined by those who were not necessarily involved in them or present when and where they occurred. In the context of the Project Approach, the documentation typically includes displays of evidence of experiences and understanding, and records and products of the activities and actions involved in the course of engagement in a project.

Documentation of project work has many possible uses and functions that can affect the learning of the children who are involved in it, as well as of their teachers. Many preschool and elementary age children interact with the display of the documented project work to revisit their own experiences and those of other classmates, read stories and narratives of pieces of work and how they were done, take a closer look at different representations, add new questions to be researched, and realize how some have been answered, as well as reflect on their own learning.

Figure 10.1   A teacher's documentation of the school bus project

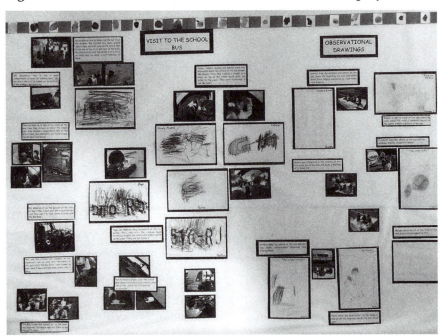

Source: Courtesy of teachers of Eton School in Mexico City.

Teachers who share their documentation with colleagues have expressed that this partaking in collegial conversations significantly contributes to their professional growth and their competence to be responsive to children's interests and needs. As teachers exchange ideas and learn from each other, they can enhance their expertise to record, interpret, follow up, and display project experiences.

In one school, teachers visit each other's classrooms during each of the three phases of a project to analyze the documentation and share ideas on where it could lead. As they brainstorm ideas, they think of different possibilities to take the project further. This manner of sharing permits them not only to hear about the experiences that have taken place but also to see how their peers display documentation.

Many teachers have reported to us that parents often gain insight concerning the nature of learning in the course of project work by examining the documentation of the experiences and the work of

Figure 10.2   A child sharing his understanding through the documentation of processes and products

Source: Courtesy of teachers of Eton School in Mexico City.

their children's class. They report their increasing awareness not only of the learning of their own children but also of deeper understandings of young children's learning and the complexities of teaching and learning in general.

OVERALL CONSIDERATIONS IN INCORPORATING DOCUMENTATION

Much about the value of documentation and the nature of displays of children's work and ideas has been learned from the preprimary schools in the northern Italian city of Reggio Emilia. Their approach to early education has been attracting worldwide attention for several decades and for many reasons (See Edwards, Gandini & Forman, 2011). Reggio Emilia documentation practices focus intensely on the children's experiences, memories, thoughts, interactions, and ideas in the course of their work of all kinds, and not only on their project activities. The children's work is displayed with great care and attention to both its content and to the aesthetic aspects of the displays. However, teachers in the pre-primary schools of Reggio Emilia typically have access to a special staff member—an *atelierista*—who is usually an experienced graphic artist and whose main responsibility is working with sub-groups of children in different classes as determined by the teaching staff. Much of the atelierista's work is helping the small groups of children with their displays for documentation. The fact that the atelierista is not the class teacher and thus not responsible for a whole class of children allows him or her to have sufficient time to produce complex and impressive displays. When classroom teachers have responsibility for the documentation of their students' work as well as for teaching the whole class, realistic expectations of how much time and effort can be given to documentation are recommended.

In some schools, administrators have explored ways to make the process of documentation possible by providing their teachers with recording devices that allow for the teacher to move around the classroom while documenting an experience. Others have mentored volunteer parents who come in during project work sessions. Some schools have arranged schedules so that teachers may work with small groups of children while sending others to alternative activities supervised by other teachers.

Documentation of the Story of the Project

The documentation of a project is likely to be most useful for all who are involved in it, as well as the parents and any other visitors, if it has a clear *narrative* quality. Whether the documentation is inside the classroom and/or on the adjacent corridor walls, viewers should easily be able to discern the story of the work, how it started and how it progressed, the development of the ideas, and the sequences of the children's experiences involved as the project developed. The narrative quality means that the documentation should include indications of the early exchanges of the children with each other and with their teachers, as well as the story of the project throughout the second and third phases of the work.

Different Kinds of Documents

Documentation includes a wide variety of media, materials, and displays. It is usually a good idea to include in the beginning sections of the documentation a copy of the original topic web created by the teacher (See Chapter 2). A topic web is usually created by the teacher as part of her planning before engaging the children in the topic. Then the teacher can develop another topic web in the course of discussions with the children (See chapters 3 & 4). A documentation display can also include transcriptions of children's conversations or of a single child's interesting comments related to the topic. Documentation can also include the children's paintings, drawings, models, and/or sculptures built in various media with a variety of materials, and photographs of events relevant to the work of the project. Some teachers videotape their students in various contexts of the project work and then make the tapes available for replay by the children as well as visitors as part of the documentation of a project.

The nature and variety of materials included in the documentation of a project would vary greatly with the ages of the participating children, of course. For toddlers, a variety of photographs and videotapes and written narratives by the teacher of experiences and conversations that she can verbally share with the children are most likely to help with documenting their experiences.

Toddlers are enthusiastic when looking at images of their project work experiences, and they are interested in listening to the stories the teacher can tell about events that took place. Some toddlers can also dictate stories that describe their graphic representations and are able to recognize their work on the display. The documentation of project work helps young children remember and re-live experiences that took place. It is important that displays are placed at a proper eye-level height, so that toddlers can interact with the documentation. As the children get older, they can create many components of the displays themselves and can engage in in-depth discussion about the advantages and disadvantages of various available types of documents.

During the first phase of the project, documentation can focus on the stories of topic-related experiences that children exchange as discussions evolve.

In the case of older students, there might be several pieces of writing and art work on display detailing memories of personal experiences related to the topic. Students can also learn from reading about the experiences of the topic their peers have had. This early exchange of ideas serves to develop interest in the topic and the curiosity necessary to provide a climate of wondering prior to developing research questions for investigation during the second phase of the project.

First-phase documentation can include materials about children's questions, ideas, predictions and hypotheses, observations and arguments concerning the topic to be investigated, and what they predict they might find out about it, depending, of course, on the ages of the children involved.

Figure 10.3   Examples of documentation and display in Phase 1

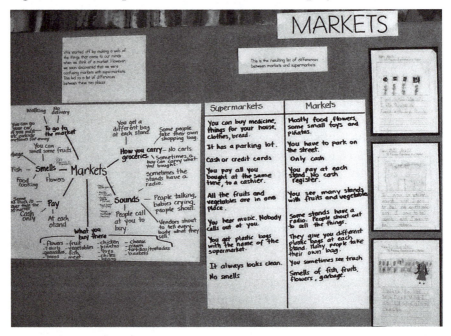

Source: Courtesy of teachers of Eton School in Mexico City.

The documentation of the participants' experiences in Phase II can include reports of their planning sessions, a few photographs of interviews the children conduct with visiting experts, their

Figure 10.4   A small table to display models

Source: Courtesy of teachers of Eton School in Mexico City.

interviews with on-site persons related to their investigations, and other experiences during site visits and field trips. Depending on the ages of the children, they can be asked to draw important objects and locations related to the main topic to be included in their displays.

Many teachers have found it useful also to encourage children to draw the same object several times, not necessarily on the same day (see Chapter 7) and to add more details and make corrections or improvements to previous drawings. In addition, the children can be encouraged to find out the names of various parts of the objects being drawn, what they are for, and how they are used. They can then add the new information into their displayed documents.

As the documentation of Phase II progresses, the teacher can take occasional opportunities to engage the children in discussions of what is thus far included in the display, especially various features in the photographs taken during the phases of the project. Teachers have frequently reported that when the children examine photographs of their experience, they often engage in serious discussions and even arguments about the nature of the events depicted. Occasionally these kinds of animated discussion require re-visiting sites and inviting an expert to return to their class to help clarify issues of interest.

Teachers have reported to us that in many cases, the parents and the larger local community have deepened their understanding and appreciation of the wide range of kinds of learning that good project work can provide.

Small tables can also be placed next to the displays with models, folders, and/or books that can include the work of individual children and samples of the work they have done in small groups, as well as relevant photographs. As the children prepare for a report to be presented to peers, schoolmates, or parents in the closing Phase III of the project, they can discuss aspects of the documentation to emphasize and highlight for their audiences.

Throughout the three phases of the project, it is often appropriate to solicit suggestions and comments from the children about the documentation on display. Their suggestions concerning what might be added or changed in some way can be a good experience for them and increase their realization that their work is taken seriously and not just sent, taken home, and pasted onto the refrigerator for three days. Such discussions can also help the teacher to understand more fully the range and variety of individual meanings children give to their work. The children can argue and disagree on various matters and can be encouraged to articulate the reasoning underlying their comments to each other. The development of the disposition to articulate and clarify one's own reasoning about important issues and to take seriously that of peers helps to build the foundation of a life-long disposition to examine one's own and others' reasoning about things that matter.

ELEVEN

The Project Approach in Perspective

The project approach is one of several educational practices intended to engage the minds of the learners at all ages. Our extensive experience of implementing the project approach with a wide range of ages of the learners strongly supports our view that good project work stimulates and supports the intellectual, social, and emotional dispositions that can substantially contribute to the capacity to lead a satisfying life—in the present as well as in the future. Because this approach to teaching and learning is so flexible, our introduction in this book is intended to serve as a guide. We know of no single or fixed way to implement the project approach. There are bound to be many variations in the elements of project work depending upon the ages of the learners, the environments in which they are being educated, and the social and political contexts in which the work is conducted.

We want to emphasize our basic definition of "projects" as in-depth investigations of phenomena and events within the children's own direct firsthand experiences. In this way, the children's education can strengthen what we hope will be a life-long disposition to seek deeper knowledge and understanding of important phenomena and events in their own experience. Furthermore, in this way, they can become most able to participate in making sound decisions for the benefit of their own environments as well as local and ultimately national decisions about what should and should not be pursued.

Not all the facts, skills, and knowledge that are important for our children to learn and master are best treated as projects. Many educational goals and topics are prescribed by the local, regional, or national authorities and must be "covered." Projects, on the other hand, are ways that topics can be "uncovered" as an investigation proceeds and takes various directions, depending on the interests and ideas of the particular group of children involved.

We have also suggested that project work is *part* of the curriculum—sometimes a large part, and sometimes a small part, depending on a variety of time, space, and curriculum constraints and opportunities. In other words, we believe that project work is a vital part of a *balanced* curriculum. As indicated in the first chapter, we see the project approach as complementary and supplementary to other aspects of the curriculum from the very early years through the elementary school years as well. Educators of children throughout children's growing years are not caught between having to choose curricula that offer *either* mainly spontaneous play plus the arts and crafts *or*, on the other hand, mainly academic formal instruction, involving drills and worksheets; neither of these two types of educational activities alone provide sufficient enrichment or challenges for children's growing minds. We do not suggest that all conventional and common academic instruction and exercises be set aside completely. Furthermore, some time should be provided for play and for the arts, etc., in the growing years for all children. In other words, a sound curriculum is one that offers ample opportunity for a range of physical activities and exposure to good literature and music, and many other commonly available experiences. In addition, children will also need carefully implemented, individual, systematic instruction to ease their way into the processes of acquiring the basic, complex skills required for competent functioning in the later school years.

Many parents and commentators who address educational issues seem to believe that unless children are engaged in formal instruction related to literacy and numeracy, they are spending their time and energy on primarily frivolous, fanciful, or mindless activities. It is our view that, in general, this view is related to a common tendency to *overestimate children academically* and to *underestimate them intellectually*. Our advocacy of the project approach is based on the assumption that when it is well done, project work provides ample contexts, pre-texts, and texts that support, stimulate, and deepen children's important *intellectual* dispositions—dispositions that are typically inborn and can be undermined by excessive and premature exposure to formal academic instruction and exercises.

Long ago, Webb (1974) framed these issues by suggesting that education must address two types of aims: *instrumental* and *intrinsic*. Instrumental aims, she suggested, assume that children are an "instrument" of society and that schooling is "an instrument" for purposes outside the school, such as preparing children for future occupations and other utilitarian and technical objectives. On the other hand, intrinsic aims deal with those aspects of learning that benefit the children themselves. These aims include valuing knowledge and understanding of phenomena around them for their own sake. These goals would also include aesthetic awareness, appreciation, and sensibilities and confidence in one's own intellectual powers. To these aims, we would also add the intellectual dispositions that are probably in-born, such as the disposition to be experimental, reflective, analytical, and critical when confronted with a range of problems and issues. Clearly, all schools for children of all ages are obliged to address both the instrumental and intrinsic aims of education. In our view, the project approach allows, and indeed supports, both kinds of aims to be addressed equally well.

In this book, we have been able to address only a few of the many topics that can be of value and interest to children. By definition, the project approach encompasses a very wide range of topics that are locally suitable and culturally relevant to the participants. One of the many challenges of incorporating projects into the curriculum is to identify topics that are appropriate for each group of children and are responsive and sensitive to salient features of their own environments. For example, project work that addresses a variety of topics and is conducted in diverse locations is described by teachers in project catalogs (see Helm, 2003). In addition, each issue of the journal *Early Childhood Research and Practice* includes a report of a project covering a very wide range of children's ages, project topics, and locations (ecrp@illinois.edu).[1]

In this third edition of *Engaging Children's Minds*, we have not—as in previous editions—included a chapter of review of relevant research. Abundant evidence continues to be reported to support the benefits of including the project approach in the curriculum throughout the years of schooling. We wish to add here that in the last dozen or so years, evidence has also been accumulating that the development of social competence must be addressed fully and effectively in at least the first six years of life, or it becomes increasingly difficult to improve it or to overcome the early difficulties experienced by some children in learning to engage competently with peers. Indeed, dropping out of school and forming strong relationships with groups we refer to as "gangs" far too frequently becomes a compensatory strategy for the formation of peer relationships based on shared bitterness and resentment for the rest of society, and it starts in the early years. Our experience with implementing the project approach throughout the school years has provided ample evidence that it not only enables the real and functional development of peer cooperation and support but also provides real contexts in which children of all ages can help each other, argue with each other, and learn from each other about the real phenomena they are investigating. They can also learn about how to help each other to document and present their findings, as well as plan, negotiate, and think collaboratively about the many possible ways to proceed with the work in which they become so absorbed.

It seems wise for us to keep in mind that virtually everything of importance in our lives involves frequent interaction with others. Indeed, the major problems we face both locally and worldwide are not simply STEM related—Scientific, Technological, Engineering, or Mathematical—they are primarily problems of a social nature requiring a long period of social skills and social disposition development in real contexts, and not just preaching. Furthermore, for all of us, it appears that the others with whom we work and interact in many different situations offer us opportunities to engage with those whose backgrounds and experiences are different from our own. Early learning of the insights, understandings, and skills involved in such diverse experiences can be easily included in many aspects of children's work in conducting the extended investigations and reporting their findings as part of project work. The quest for solutions to these socially based problems will undoubtedly continue for decades to come—when today's children have become tomorrow's adults.

As we have already suggested throughout this book, the project approach, as we see it, gives teachers the opportunity to attend equally to social *and* intellectual development. Decision-makers who are intent upon school reform rarely hesitate to cry out that improvements in education are necessary to cope with the economic and technological exigencies of the future. Early and frequent experience of working cooperatively on mind-engaging tasks can also improve the chances of being able to cope well with the complex social issues of today, as well as those likely to challenge our children as they grow up and grow older.

It may be a propitious moment in time to return to the proverbial drawing board and develop methods for assessing the potential benefits of good project work. Besides giving grades or other extrinsic rewards, there should be other ways to assess the effectiveness of practices that strengthen desirable dispositions, such as children's eagerness to work, to persist, to find out things, and to overcome setbacks as they proceed with their work. Their motivation and level of interest in their project investigations, their evident willingness to come to school, their general cooperativeness, and peer interactive competences, alongside developing basic literacy, numeracy, and other academic skills should be closely observed by teachers and parents and other educators to help us learn to improve our methods of fully engaging children. Our extensive experience with the project approach has included many occasions when teachers and parents have expressed their amazement about how motivated their children are when engaged in projects.

To date, the evidence of the benefits of the project approach is primarily indirect rather than careful, systematic, and controlled comparative longitudinal studies. However, like every curriculum approach, the project approach can be implemented at various levels of effectiveness. When well done, we suggest that it can address *all* aspects of children's development and learning. Until such good evidence is available, we want to encourage teachers themselves to experiment with the project approach and use documentation strategies to deepen their own awareness of the learning that has been facilitated or perhaps overlooked. We are eager to hear about these experiments and see the documentations of children's work.

In the last two plus decades since the publication of our first edition of this book, we have already been privileged to learn a great deal from firsthand accounts of teachers' professional development as they have communicated with us about the project work they have undertaken all over the world. For many teachers, the project approach seemed to be very complex at first. But we now know a great deal more about how to include and support children with a range of special needs into project activities. Projects are easier for some teachers to implement than for others, for a wide variety of reasons. These individual differences may be related to teachers' prior teaching philosophies, practices, and experiences or to the institutional, collegial, or administrative contexts in which they work.

SUMMARY

As already indicated, we have learned that both teachers and children of all ages sometimes take time to feel comfortable with the strategies and skills necessary to develop productive projects. We have learned from some teachers just embarking on the project approach that it can help to begin slowly, to investigate smaller-scale topics, sometimes referred to as "mini-projects," on topics such as "sunflowers in our outdoors," "the shop next door to our school," or "the people in our class." Older children often appear to have already learned to be passive in the classroom. They are challenged at first when a teacher begins to involve them more directly in planning, developing, and evaluating their own work. On the other hand, because most of the older children have more representational skills available than younger ones to apply to their project work and potentially greater communicative competence, it does not take long before they "take over" the project.

We look forward to continuing to learn from teachers who are personally experiencing the very real and direct advantages of projects to the children they work with. We also hope to be able to offer support to teachers experiencing doubts or difficulties. We have learned that sometimes the most useful help for teachers is that which is provided to them by other teachers.

Our experience of working with teachers all over the world as they incorporate project work in their curriculum supports our conviction that when it is well done, it engages the growing minds of children in ways that develop and strengthen the most important dispositions and feelings: the dispositions to seek understanding and knowledge of significant phenomena around them and to deepen their feelings of enjoying helping and cooperating with their peers. In addition, good project work involves investigations of worthwhile topics that provide contexts for the construction, acquisition, and strengthening of basic, important, and useful academic skills and knowledge of important use throughout life.

A Wide Range of Information and Access to Publications can be downloaded from:
ILLINOIS PROJECTS IN PRACTICE
PIP-L@LISTSERVE.ILLINOIS.EDU

NOTE

1. The journal *Early Childhood Research & Practice* (<u>ECRP@illinois.edu</u>) can be downloaded free of charge.

References

Alexander, P. A., K. Murphy, and B. S. Woods. (1996, April). "Of ISqualls and Fathoms: Navigating the Seas of Educational Innovation." *Educational Researcher* 23(3): 31–39.

Beneke, S. (1998). *Rearview Mirror: Reflections on a Preschool Car Project.* Champaign, IL: ERIC Clearinghouse on Elementary and Early Childhood Education.

Blair, C. (2010). "Stress and the Development of Self-regulation in Context." *Child Development Perspectives* 4(3): 181–188.

Blank., M. (1985). "Classroom Discourse: The Neglected Topic of the Topic." In M. M. Clark (Ed.), *Helping Communication in Early Education* (pp. 13–20). *Educational Review Occasional Publication No. 11.* Birmingham, England: University of Birmingham. UK.

Dearden, R. F. (1984). *Theory and Practice in Education.* London: Routledge & Kegan Paul.

Dewey, J. (1904). "The Relation of Theory to Practice in Education." In *Third Yearbook of the National Society for the Scientific Study of Education.* Chicago: University of Chicago Press.

Dresden, J. & K. Lee. (2007). "The Effects of Project Work in a First Grade Classroom: A Little Goes a Long Way." http://www.ecrp.uiuc.edu/v9n1/dresden.html.

Edwards, B. (2012 [1979]). *Drawing on the Right Side of the Brain: A Course in Enhancing Creativity and Artistic Confidence.* New York: J. P. Tarcher.

Edwards, L. Gandini, and G. Forman (1998). *The Hundred Languages of Children: The Reggio Emilia Approach—Advanced Reflections.* 2nd Edition. Stamford, CT: Ablex.

Edwards, C. P., L. Gandini, and G. Forman (2011). *The Hundred Languages of Children: The Reggio Emilia Experience in Transformation.* 3rd Edition. Santa Barbara, CA: Praeger.

Forman, George (1993). *Jed Draws His Bicycle: A Case of Drawing-to-Learn.* Videotape. Available from Performanetics, 19 The Hollow, Amherst, MA 01002.

Fyfe, Brenda (2011). "The Relationship between Documentation and Assessment." In Edwards, C., L. Gandini, and G. Forman (Eds.) *The Hundred Languages of Children.* Santa Barbara, CA: Praeger.

Gallas, K. (1994). *The Language of Learning: How Children Talk, Write, Dance, Draw, and Sing Their Understanding of the World.* New York: Teachers College Press.

Gandini, L., S. Eteredge, and L. Hill. (2008) *Insights and Inspirations from Reggio Emilia.* Worcester, MA: Davis Pub.

Gardner, D., and J. Cass. (1965). *The Role of the Teacher in the Infant and Nursery School.* NY: Pergamon Press.

Goodnow, J. J. (1977). *Children Drawing.* Cambridge, MA: Harvard U. Pr.

Harkema, R. (1999) "The School Bus Project." In *Early Childhood Research & Practice.* Available: http://ecrp.uiuc.edu/v1n2/harkema.html [November, 1999]

Helm, J. H. (Ed.). (2000). "The Project Approach Catalog 3." Urbana, IL: *ERIC Clearinghouse on Early Childhood Education.*

Helm, J. H. (Ed.). (2003). "The Project Approach Catalog 4: Literacy and Project Work." *Early Childhood and Parenting Collaborative.* Urbana, IL: University of Illinois.

Helm, J. H. & L. G. Katz. (2011). "Young Investigators." *The Project Approach in the Early Years.* 2nd Edition. NY, NY: Teachers College Press.

Helm, J. H., S. Beneke, and K. Steinheimer. (2007). "Windows on Learning." *Documenting Young Children's Work.* 2nd Edition. NY: Teachers College Press.

Hinchman, H. (1997). *A Trail through Leaves: The Journal as a Path to Place.* New York: W. W. Norton.

Hinchman, H. 1991. *A Life in Hand: Creating the Illuminated Journal.* Gibbs Smith pub.

Illinois State Board of Education (2002). *Illinois Standards for Childhood 3 to 5.* State Department of Education. Springfield, Illinois.

Isaacs, S. (1966). *Intellectual Growth in Young Children*: London, UK: Schocken Books.

Katz, L. G. (1995). *Talks with Teachers of Young Children: A Collection.* Norwood, NJ: Ablex.

Katz, Lilian G. (1999) "All About Balls: A Preschool Project." ERIC Clearinghouse on Elementary & Early Childhood Education. University of Illinois. 61820—7469.

Katz, L. G. (2012). "Distinctions between Academic Versus Intellectual Goals for Young Children." *NYSAEC Reporter* 39(2) (Winter): 1–15.

Katz, L. G. & B. Cesarone. (Eds.) (1994). *Reflections on the Reggio Emilia Approach.* Urbana, IL: ERIC Clearinghouse on Elementary & Early Childhood Education.

Katz, L. G., D. Evangelou, and J. Hartman. (1990). *The Case for Mixed-Age Grouping in the Early Years.* Washington, D. C.: National Association for the Education of Young Children.

Keats, E. J. (1998 [1968]). *A Letter to Amy.* Viking Juvenile.

Kendall, J. (2011). *Understanding Common Core State Standards.* Alexandria, VA: Association for Supervision & Curriculum Development.

Kilpatrick, W. H. (1918). "The Project Method." *Teachers College Record* 19: 319–334.

Kliebard, H. M. (1985). "What Happened to American Schooling in the First Part of the Twentieth Century?" In Eisner, E. (Ed.). *Learning and Teaching the Ways of Knowing.* Pp. 1–22. Chicago: University of Chicago Press.

Kogan, Y., and J. Pin (2009). "Beginning the Journey: The Project Approach with Toddlers." http://ecrp.uiuc.edu

London, P. (1989). *No More Second-Hand Art: Awakening the Artist Within.* Boston: Shambhala.

Marcon, R. (2002). "Relationship between Preschool Model and Later School Success." www.ecrp.uiuc.edu/v4n1/marcon.html

Moline, S. (1995). *I See What You Mean: Children at Work with Visual Information.* York, ME: Stenhouse.

Nelson, K. (1986). *Event Knowledge: Structure and Function in Development.* Hilldale, NJ: Lawrence Erlbaum.

New, R. (2005). "The Reggio Approach: Provocations and Partnerships with U. S. Early Childhood Education." In Jaipaul, R. & J. E. Johnson, (Eds.). *Approaches to Early Childhood Education* (6th Edition). New Jersey: Pearson Education Upper Saddle River.

Nidi e Scuole Communali dell'Infanzia di Reggio Emilia (1997) *Shoe and Meter.* Commune di Reggio Emilia, Italy.

Nisbett, R. E., A. Aronson, C. Blair, et al. (2012). "Intelligence: New Findings and Theoretical Developments." *American Psychologist* 67(2): 130–159.

Plowden Committee Report (1967). *Children and their Primary Schools.* London, UK: Her Majesty's Stationary Office.

Prawat, R. S. (1995). "Misreading Dewey: Reform, Projects and the Language Game." *Educational Researcher* 24 (7): 12–22.

Ravitch, D. (2013). *Reign of Error. The Hoax of the Privatization Movement and the Danger to America's Public Schools.* New York: Alfred A. Knopf.

Rothman, R. (2013). "Diving into Deeper Learning. Schools Gear Up to Promote Thinking Skills." *Harvard Education Letter* (March/April) 29(2): 1-3.

Ruef, K. (1994). *The Private Eye (5X) Looking: Thinking by Analogy—A Guide to Developing the Interdisciplinary Mind*. Seattle, WA: The Private Eye Project.

Schuler, Dot (2012). *Just Ask the Children* (Published by author).

Stevahn, L., D. W. Johnson, R. Johnson, et al. (1996). "The Impact of a Cooperative or Individualistic Context on the Effectiveness of Conflict Resolution Training." *American Educational Research Journal* (Winter) 33(4): 801–823.

Stewart, J. (1986). *The Making of the Primary School*. Milton Keynes, England: Open University Press.

Tomlinson, C. A. (2008). "The Goals of Differentiation." *Journal of Educational Leadership*. 66(3): 26–30.

Van Ausdal, S. J. (1988). "William Heard Kilpatrick: Philosopher and Teacher." *Childhood Education* 68(3): 164–168.

Wanerman, T. (2013). *From Handprints to Hypotheses: Using the Project Approach with Toddlers and Twos*. St. Paul, MN: Redleaf Press.

Webb., L. (1974). *Purpose and Practice in Nursery Education*. Oxford, UK: Basil Blackwell.

Wilson, P. S. (1971). *Interest and the Discipline of Education*. London: Routledge & Kegan Paul.

Yeager, D. S. & C. S. Dweck. (2012). "Mindsets that Promote Resilience: When Students Believe that Personal Characteristics can be Developed." *Educational Psychologist* 47(4): 302–314.

Zhao, Xu, H. Haste, and R. L. Selman. (2014). "Questionable Lessons from China's Recent History of Education Reform." *Education Week* (January 22): 32.

Zimilies, H. (1997). "Viewing Education through a Psychological Lens: The contributions of Barbara Biber." *Child Psychiatry and Human Development* 28: 23–31.

Subject Index

A

abilities: age and, 19; drawing, 123, 128, 129; groupings by, 93; intellectual abilities of children, 11–12, 212; products of work and, 88

academic curriculum, 10

accountability: with parents, 75; pressures for, 61–62

activities: for the children, 38–39; consolidation activities, 100–101; construction activities, 85–86; culminating activity, 169–171; dramatic play, 87–88; for first phase of extended projects, 71–74; investigation activities, 86–87; for learning, 85–88; open house, 101; preschoolers and, 13, 18; products of work, 88; supplementary, 102; for toddlers, 134

activities, balancing various, 12–13; academic vs. creative curriculum, 13; formal instruction, 13; project work benefits, 12–13; small-group instruction, 13; whole-class formal instruction, 13

aesthetics, 110

ages of children for project approach, 18–19

aims of education, 9, 12, 213

aims of project approach, 9–10; child development, 9; "mind" term defined, 9; overall aim, 9; recommendation for, 10

American Civil War, 187

art: expressive/impressionistic, 120; media, 73; systematic instruction in, 110; techniques, 129. *See also* drawing

audience, 89, 99

B

balanced curriculum, 7, 10, 13, 212

bar graphs, 89

basic skills: application of, 39, 41, 85; appreciation of, 46; formal instruction in, 13, 212

behavioral knowledge, 40–41

Blank, Jolyn, 112

books: class books at concluding phase, 26; *Drawing on the Right Side of the Brain* (Edward), 128; illustrations in, 129; *A Letter to Amy* (Keats, 1968), 69; *A Life in Hand* (Hinchman), 128; secondary sources of information, 4, 30, 82; *A Trail through Leaves* (Hinchman), 128

boredom, 97

Author Index

Please note entries in *italic* indicate references.

A

Alexander, P. A., Murphy, K., & Woods, B. S., 6, *219*

B

Blair, C., 7, *219*
Blank., M., 36, *219*

C

Chard, Sylvia C., 223

D

Dearden, R. F., 6, *219*
Dewey, John, 5, *219*
Dresden, J. & Lee, Kyunghwa, 7, *219*

E

Edwards, B., 128, *219*
Edwards, C. P., Gandini, L., Forman, G., 11, 205, *219*

F

Forman, George, 117, *220*

G

Gallas, K., 28, 111, *220*

Gandini, L., Etheredge, S., & Hill, L., 5, *220*

H

Helm, J. H., Beneke, S. Steinheimer, K., 69, 73, 96, *220*
Hinchman, H., 131, *220*

I

Isaacs, Susan, 6, *220*

K

Katz, L. G., 6, 12, *220*
Katz, L. G. & Cesarone, B., 11, *220*
Katz, L. G., Evangelou, D., Hartman, J., 19, *220*
Katz, Lilian G., 223
Kendall, John, 10, *221*
Kilpatrick, William H., 5, *221*
Kliebard, H. M., 6, 54, *221*
Kogan, Y., Pin, J., 5, *221*
Kogan, Yvonne, 223

L

London, P., 119, *221*

About the Authors

Sylvia C. Chard, PhD, is professor emeritus of Elementary Education at the University of Alberta, Edmonton, Alberta, Canada. Her published works include *Engaging Children's Minds: The Project Approach*, co-authored with Lilian G. Katz (1989, 2000), and *The Project Approach: A Practical Guide for Teachers*, Vols. 1 & 2 (Scholastic, 1998). She maintains a website with teacher resources on the Project Approach at www.projectapproach.org. Chard holds a doctorate in education from the University of Illinois.

Lilian G. Katz, PhD, is professor emerita and member of staff of the Clearinghouse on Early Education & Parents at the University of Illinois, Urbana-Champaign. Dr. Katz worked several years as a nursery school teacher before earning her PhD at Stanford University. Dr. Katz has published numerous articles, chapters, and books about early education, parenting, and teacher education. She has lectured on these topics in 55 countries.

Yvonne Kogan, M.Ed., is the co-owner and head principal of the Early Childhood and Elementary Departments of Eton School in Mexico City. She is also a consultant for numerous schools in Mexico. Kogan has published several articles on the Project Approach and is the co-author, with Dr. Sylvia C. Chard, of the book entitled *From My Side: Being a Child*